Wee-Built Bible Town

13 Preschool Lessons That Build Faith in Jesus

Group

Loveland, Colorado

Group's R.E.A.L. Guarantee to you:

Every Group resource incorporates our R.E.A.L. approach to ministry—a unique philosophy that results in long-term retention and life transformation. It's ministry that's:

This is EARL. He's R.E.A.L. mixed up. (Get it?)

Relational
Because student-to-student interaction enhances learning and builds Christian friendships.

Experiential
Because what students experience sticks with them up to 9 times longer than what they simply hear or read.

Applicable
Because the aim of Christian education is to be both hearers and doers of the Word.

Learner-based
Because students learn more and retain it longer when the process is designed according to how they learn best.

Wee-Built Bible Town: 13 Preschool Lessons That Build Faith in Jesus
Copyright © 2001 Group Publishing, Inc.

Visit our Web site: **www.grouppublishing.com**

Credits
Contributing Authors: Sharon Carey, Robin Christy, Diane Cory, Neil Dyer, and Nancy Wendland Feehrer
Editor: Linda A. Anderson
Creative Development Editor: Jody Brolsma
Chief Creative Officer: Joani Schultz
Copy Editor: Pam Klein
Art Director: Kari K. Monson
Cover Art Director: Jeff A. Storm
Cover Illustrator: Karen Lee
Computer Graphic Artist: Stephen Beer
Illustrators: Shelley Dieterichs, Cathy Ann Johnson, and Nancy Munger
Production Manager: Peggy Naylor

ISBN 0-7644-2231-6

10 9 8 7 6 5 4 3 2 1   10 09 08 07 06 05 04 03 02 01

Printed in the United States of America.

Contents

Introduction

Delightful, joyous, energetic, curious, fun-loving—your preschoolers! These precious three- to five-year-olds can learn so much, especially if they are learning by doing. *Wee-Built Bible Town* provides age-appropriate, hands-on projects and lessons that will immerse your children in life during biblical times. Helping children connect Jesus' life and culture with their own experiences is a wonderful way to capture children's hearts.

Each of the thirteen lessons is designed to appeal to all of children's learning styles and all of the senses. In each lesson, the children will build a component of a Bible-times village, and at the same time, kids will learn a powerful lesson about Jesus. By the time you have completed all thirteen lessons, you will have transformed your classroom into a complete Bible-town experience and built faith in Jesus. You can do the lessons in any order that works for you.

Preschoolers feel happier and more secure when they have a familiar routine. So we've structured each lesson to include the following elements.

The Foundation—The point of the lesson and the Scripture reference.

The Background—Background information about the aspect of village life that the lesson will cover.

The Tools—A list of the materials you'll need to complete the lesson.

The Excavation—The preparation you'll have to do before the lesson.

The Project—The lesson itself, which is broken down into the following six elements.

- **Ribbon-Cutting**—A brief attention-grabbing activity to introduce the lesson.

- **Whistle While You Work**—A short song to reinforce the point of the lesson or to sing with your children while you build the village component.

- **Blueprint**—The segment in which children learn the Bible story.

- **Framework**—During this activity, the children will help build a component of the village and connect it to the life of Jesus and to the point of the lesson.

- **Builders Banquet**—A simple snack that relates to the lesson.

- **Dedication**—This is the closing activity that always includes a prayer.

Additions—Other activities and games for you to use as you have time.

Plus there's a Bible-Town Take-Home Page that you can make copies of for kids to take home. The take-home pages provide fun activities for the children to do at home with their families to help kids remember what they've learned.

Use this resource to provide your preschoolers with an experience they'll never forget and to help them develop a new love and appreciation for Jesus.

A Different Kind of House

Housing in Bible Times

The Foundation

Jesus is more important than anything else.

Luke 10:38-42

The Background

In biblical times, most houses were built in the cities. Farmers, too, often lived in the cities, although they would stay out in their fields during harvest time. Houses in the cities were usually built close together to conserve space, and they had walls of mud bricks or rough stones and floors of clay. To conserve heat in the winter and to keep the temperature cool in the summer, houses had few windows, and they rarely had windows on the ground floor.

Houses were used for many different purposes in Bible times. They were places to live, places to worship, storerooms, barns, and workplaces. Houses often had courtyards that were used as cooking areas and for housing some of the more valuable animals in the winter.

Houses often had two stories, and people used ladders or stairs to climb up to the main living and sleeping rooms. The roofs were flat and were made by covering beams with branches and a layer of mud plaster. The family could sleep on the roof in the summer or use the space to dry fruits or grains.

Jesus used the metaphor of building a house on a solid foundation to show how important it was for people to put his words into practice (see Matthew 7:24-27). This idea may have had greater impact on Jesus' audience because they lived in an area that was prone to earthquakes. Isaiah prophesied that Jesus would be "a precious cornerstone for a sure foundation" (Isaiah 28:16-19). Indeed, Jesus is the only worthwhile foundation on which we can build our lives—Jesus is more important than anything else.

The Tools

- Bible
- refrigerator box

- packing tape
- utility knife
- markers
- newsprint
- masking tape
- 10-12 large stones or pieces of gray bulletin board paper crumpled into rock shapes
- red tissue paper
- old sheets or towels
- a disposable 6-muffin tin for each child
- wheat crackers
- apple slices
- pita bread triangles
- applesauce
- hummus
- peanut butter

The Excavation

Take a refrigerator box, and tape the ends shut with packing tape. Set the box on one of its long sides, and use a utility knife to cut along the sides and top edge of the front panel of the box. Fold the front flap down to create a "courtyard" as shown in the illustration.

Use a marker to draw a circle in the middle of the courtyard where the "fire pit" will be. The children will help you create the fire pit later.

The Project

Ribbon-Cutting

Ask each child to describe the house where he or she lives. Then have children use markers to draw their homes on sheets of newsprint.

When kids have finished, say: **In Bible times, the houses looked different than most of our houses look today. We're going to learn about houses in Bible times and build our very own Bible-times house. We'll also discover that no matter where you live, Jesus is always with you!**

Whistle While You Work

Have the children stand up. Teach kids this song to the tune of "Home on the Range," and encourage them to do the motions.

Bible-Town Tip

You may wish to cover the box with brown craft paper or paint the box with brown tempera paint to simulate mud bricks. If you have time, the children can help with this step.

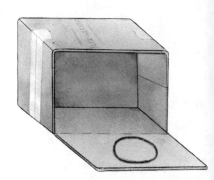

Sing

Oh, this is my home (*use hands to form the pointed roof of a house*),
Where I know I can roam. (*Take a few sauntering steps.*)
Where I can sing and dance and play. (*Lift hands in the air and spin around.*)
I don't have to fear (*pretend to bite nails*),
Because Jesus is near (*hug self*);
And he's with me ev-er-y-day. (*Lift arms in praise.*)

Blueprint

Ask the children to sit on the floor in a circle. Say: **In Bible times, the houses looked different than most of our houses look today. Back then, the houses were built very close together, and they had flat roofs! Let's make some houses with our bodies to see the difference. We'll start by building a neighborhood like many of the ones we see today.**

Have the children stand in a line. Ask the first two children to face each other and hold hands. Have them form a slanted "roof" by raising their arms up. Then let the other children in the line make a row of "houses," with space between them to represent the yards.

Say: **In many of our neighborhoods today, houses have slanted roofs and have some space between them for our yards. Back in Bible times, the houses were close together, like they are in some of our big cities, and the houses had flat roofs where people could sleep in the summer. Now let's make a Bible-times neighborhood.**

As the children stand in a line, have kids form pairs facing each other and holding hands. Now have kids form houses with flat roofs by extending their arms straight out and bending their heads down. Encourage kids to keep these Bible-times houses close together.

Then have the children sit on the floor. Open your Bible to Luke 10:38-42, and show kids the words. Say: **Jesus and his good friends were traveling one day, and they came to a small town. In the town lived two sisters named Mary and Martha. Mary and Martha asked Jesus to come to Martha's house.** Ask:

• **Have you ever had important people come to your house?**

• **What did you have to do to get the house ready for the visitors?**

If the children have trouble thinking of ideas, give some suggestions, such as picking up all the toys or cooking a big meal. Have the kids act out the activities that the other children have suggested.

Say: **Those are some of the things that Martha did to get her house ready. In fact, Martha was still working hard while Jesus was in her house talking to Mary. But Mary just sat and listened to Jesus. Can you show me what Mary did?** Encourage the children to sit quietly.

Martha became very angry that her sister wasn't working hard like she was. Martha thought that it wasn't fair for Mary to just sit and listen to Jesus. Martha asked Jesus to have Mary help her with the work. But Jesus said that it was better to listen to him. And Jesus still wants us to listen to him today. Remember, Jesus is more important than anything else.

It was a very special thing to have Jesus come to visit. Ask:

• **What things would you do if Jesus was coming to visit *your* house?**

Say: **Jesus is with you all the time. He's a special visitor in your home. No matter what kind of house you live in, Jesus is there with you.**

Framework

Say: **Today we're going to use a box to build a house—a house kind of like the one Jesus might have gone to when he visited Mary and Martha.**

First you'll want to put "bricks" on the outside of the house. Direct children to use masking tape to make brick outlines on the refrigerator box. Have kids take strips of masking tape and tape them horizontally along the sides of the box, with about 6 to 8 inches between the strips. Then let the children put shorter strips of masking tape vertically between the long strips to make bricks about 8 inches long. You may want to draw lines on the box with a marker for the children to follow, but it's OK if the bricks aren't perfectly rectangular! Remember that in Bible times, bricks were made from straw and mud and probably were not perfectly shaped either.

Next have the children make the "fire pit." Let the children place stones or crumpled pieces of paper in the circle you drew earlier on the box. Then have kids wad up red tissue paper and put it in the circle to represent a fire.

Set out one sleeping mat for each child. These can be old towels or sheets cut into rectangles.

Builders Banquet

A meal in biblical times may have included some of the following foods: wheat bread, figs, apples, pomegranates, olives, cucumbers, lentils, and raisins.

It's important that you know if the children in your class have allergies to the foods you serve them. Some children, for example, could have lethal reactions to peanut butter.

People usually ate their food with their fingers, sometimes using pieces of bread to scoop up sauces or other foods.

Before you begin, have kids wash their hands. Then try serving this tasty, scoopable snack. Use one 6-muffin tin for each child. (Disposable aluminum-foil tins are available at most grocery stores.) In three of the cups, put wheat crackers, apple slices, and pita bread triangles. In the other three spaces put applesauce, hummus, and peanut butter. Pray and ask God to bless the snacks, then let the kids dip their tasty treats and eat with their fingers. Hold your banquet around the fire in the courtyard of your new Bible-times house!

Dedication

Gather near your Bible-times house and dedicate it to God.

Say: **To dedicate something means to set it apart or save it for something special. God wants us to "set apart" our homes and lives to serve him!**

Have kids stand in a circle. Hold hands and say this prayer:

Dear God,

We dedicate this Bible-times house to you! We pray that this house will remind us that you sent Jesus to live on earth and that Jesus is more important than anything else. Help us to remember you are always with us—in our homes and everywhere!

In Jesus' name, amen.

After your dedication, you may wish to let kids each get out a sleeping mat and pretend to take a nap!

Additions

• At one end of the house, you may want to put "stairs" that lead up to the flat roof. (Remind the kids *not* to climb these stairs!) Wrap small boxes or shoe boxes in brown paper. Stack the boxes at one end of the house, and tape or glue them together.

• People in biblical times often dried fruits and grains on the roofs. You may want to have children use strips of yellow construction paper to represent flax or wheat stalks and set these on the roof.

• The roof was also used as a sleeping area in hot weather, and you may want to put a couple of your sleeping mats on the roof as well. Remind kids not to climb up on the roof.

• Try your hand at making bricks! Start by making some salt dough. In a bowl, mix 1 cup of salt with 1 cup of flour and enough water to moisten the ingredients to form dough. (This will make enough dough for four children.) Give each child a bowl with some salt dough in it. Then give each child ¼ cup of dried chopped straw or hay. (Craft stores often sell decorative straw.) Ask the children to become brickmakers by mixing the straw into the dough. When the dough is fully mixed, ask the children to use the dough to form miniature bricks. Challenge kids to use their bricks to create a small house or fire pit. You may also want to let kids use all of their bricks to make a house together as a whole class. The dough will air-dry in a day or two.

Bible-Town Take-Home Page

Today kids heard the story of Jesus' visit to Mary and Martha (Luke 10:38-42), and they learned that Jesus is more important than anything else. Children also learned about the types of houses that people lived in during biblical times. You can build on this lesson by helping your child make a miniature Bible-times house.

House: Take the lid off of a shoe box, and set the box on its side behind the lid. This will be the house and the courtyard. You may wish to have your child tape the box to the lid to secure it. Have your child paint or color the outside of the box brown, and help your child use a black crayon or marker to draw small mud bricks on the walls. Then work with your child to add some or all of the following features to your Bible-times house.

Fire Pit: Gather small stones to make a fire pit, and glue them together in a circle in the courtyard. Cut out a piece of thin cardboard in the shape of a flame. Spread glue onto the cardboard, sprinkle red glitter onto the glue, and allow the glue to dry. Then put a piece of clay or modeling dough in the center of the fire pit, and press the cardboard into the clay to make the fire.

Sleeping Mats: Cut a piece of cloth into small rectangles, and use markers to decorate the sleeping mats. Be sure to put some of the mats on the roof for summer sleeping!

Food Drying: Cut out small rectangles of paper, and glue raisins, barley, or other grains to the papers. Glue the paper rectangles on the roof of the house to represent food drying.

12

Cloak of Kindness

Clothing in Bible Times

The Background

Clothing is mentioned in the Bible all the way back in Genesis. Clothing is first associated with Adam and Eve and the shame they felt when they realized that they were naked. In Genesis 3:21, read about how God made clothes for Adam and Eve out of skins. (Talk about designer clothing!)

In biblical times, clothing was not made primarily for its looks, but rather for its function. Clothes were influenced by the climate and were meant to provide ease of movement. Clothes for men and women were very similar, although the Bible says in Deuteronomy 22:5 that women must not wear men's clothing and men must not wear women's clothing.

Common types of clothing in biblical times were shirts, cloaks, belts, head coverings, and sandals. The shirt or tunic could be short or long—sometimes all the way down to the ankles. It might be made of linen or wool, and it could have short sleeves, long sleeves, or no sleeves. Sometimes people would lift up the bottom of a long shirt so that they could run. Almost everyone had a cloak, which was basically a large piece of cloth that was thrown over one or both shoulders and had openings for the arms. It was used at night as a blanket and was also used to carry items.

People also wore folded squares of cloth as veils for protection against the sun or wrapped around their heads as turbans. The belt was a folded piece of cloth that could be used to hold money or other valuables.

Shoes were basically sandals made of leather or wood and tied with thongs. Sandals were not worn inside the houses, and poor people often went barefoot.

In this lesson, children will learn about clothes in biblical times and will discover that God wants us to be kind and caring like Jesus.

The Tools

- Bible
- refrigerator box
- packing tape
- utility knife
- adhesive-backed clothing hooks
- adult-sized biblical costume including a long shirt, cloak, belt, head covering, and sandals
- a clean, oversized, plain T-shirt for each child
- scissors
- enough fabric to make a 2- by 5-foot cloak for each child
- enough fabric to make a 4-inch by 4-foot belt for each child
- markers, fabric paint, fake jewels, and ribbons
- fabric glue
- people-shaped gingerbread cookies
- fruit leather
- thin licorice
- napkins

The Excavation

Take a refrigerator box and seal the top and bottom with clear packing tape. Using a utility knife, cut a door on one side to make a dressing room. Fold the door back and forth several times to make the "hinge" on the uncut side work smoothly so that the door will open and close easily. Inside the box, attach adhesive-backed clothing hooks to the walls.

Cut the fabric for the cloaks. Each piece should be about 2 feet by 5 feet. Then cut the fabric for the belts. Each belt should be about 4 inches by 4 feet.

The Project

Ribbon-Cutting

Ask the children to sit in a circle. Play a game in which the children will stand up if they are wearing a certain type of clothing. For example, you might say, "Stand up if you are wearing a T-shirt" or "Stand up if you are wearing a dress." Ask:

- **Why do you wear clothes?**
- **Can you think of other reasons that people might wear clothes?**

Some answers could be that people wear clothes to keep warm, to cover up, to protect themselves during various activities, or even to impress others.

Say: **In Bible times people wore clothing, but it didn't look like the clothing we wear now. Today we'll learn about Bible-times clothing and make some clothes like the kind that people wore back then. While I go and change my clothes in our dressing room, get with a partner and see how many kinds of clothing you can think of.**

Have kids form pairs, and give them a few examples to start with. Then quickly go into the dressing room and put on your costume. When you return, ask:

- **What types of clothing did you and your partner think of?**

- **Am I wearing any of the clothing that you thought of?**

- **How are my clothes different from your clothes?**

Say: **The clothes I have on are like the clothes Jesus might have worn. Clothes are important and we all wear them, but in the Bible God tells us not to be worried about what we wear. God cares that we have clothes to wear on the outside of us, but he cares more about what we are like on the inside. He wants us to have a good heart on the inside, and he wants us to be kind and caring like Jesus.**

Whistle While You Work

Teach children this song to the tune of "The Farmer in the Dell." Let kids sing it later as they decorate the shirts.

Sing

We can show we care.
Caring means we share.
God will be so proud of us,
When we show we care.

Kindness is the way,
The way to act all day.
God will be so proud of us,
'Cause kindness is the way.

We'll clothe ourselves with love.
We'll clothe ourselves with love.
God will be so proud of us.
We'll clothe ourselves with love.

Blueprint

Have the children sit together in a circle.

Say: **The word** *clothe* **means to cover; our clothes cover our bodies. Today, we're going to learn about clothing in Bible times.**

Clothes today are very different from the clothes people wore in Bible times. Back then, people wore clothes that protected them from the weather and that were easy to move in instead of wearing things just because they looked good.

The Bible talks about clothing all the way back to the very beginning in the book of Genesis, which is the first book of the Bible. The Bible says that God made Adam and Eve their first clothes. Isn't that amazing!

In the time when Jesus lived, people wore a type of shirt called a tunic. It could have long sleeves or short sleeves, and it could be long or short in length. Point out the part of your costume that is like a tunic. **People also wore something called a cloak. A cloak went over a person's shirt—sort of like a jacket.** Point out the cloak that you're wearing. **In Bible times, people also wore a type of veil or head covering, a belt, and sandals on their feet.** Point out these items to the children.

In one story in the Bible, a woman who was very sick reached out and touched Jesus' cloak. Open your Bible to Luke 8:42b-48, and show kids the words.

Jesus had been walking down the street in a big crowd of people. Let's pretend that I'm Jesus and all of you are in the crowd of people all around me. Choose one child to be the sick woman. Gather all the children closely around you and move as a group across the room. Have the child who is the sick woman try to reach in and touch the bottom of your cloak. Do this several times, allowing different children to be the sick woman. Ask:

• **Was it easy or hard to touch the bottom of my cloak?**

• **Do you think it would have been easy or hard for the sick woman in the Bible to reach Jesus and touch his cloak?**

• **What do you think happened when the woman touched Jesus' cloak?**

Say: **Jesus knew that the woman needed to be healed—and she** *was* **healed! Jesus was kind and caring toward the woman.** Ask:

• **How do you feel when someone is kind to you?**

• **What are some kind things you could do for someone?**

• **Who is someone you can be kind to?**

Say: **Even if you don't have clothes like Jesus, you can be kind and caring** like Jesus was. Covering or clothing ourselves is important, but God wants us to remember that it's even more important for us to try to be kind and caring like Jesus.

Framework

Have kids each decorate a shirt. Set out markers and fabric paint on a table, and have the children sit or stand around a table. Set the jewels, ribbons, and glue on the table as well.

Hand out a shirt to each child. Help kids each put their shirt on the table with the front side up. Use a permanent marker to write children's names on the bottom edge of their shirts. Then have kids use the materials on the table to decorate the shirts.

Give children each a belt and a cloak, and tell them that they can try on their clothing after snack time. Remind kids that Jesus was kind when he healed the sick woman who touched his cloak. Tell children that their Bible-times clothing can remind them to be kind and caring too.

Builders Banquet

Before you begin, have kids wash their hands. Give each child a napkin and a gingerbread man. (The cookies can be homemade or purchased.) Next, give each child a strip of fruit leather and a piece of thin licorice. Kids will use the fruit leather and licorice to make shirts and belts for their gingerbread people. (The size of each piece depends on the size of the gingerbread men. You may need to experiment to see how long to make the strips of fruit leather and licorice.)

Help the children each fold the fruit leather in half and tear along the fold halfway across so that they can slip the fruit leather shirt over the head of the gingerbread person. Then let kids each tie a licorice belt around the gingerbread cookie's waist. Younger preschoolers may need help with this step.

Thank God for the snacks, then eat and enjoy the treats!

Dedication

Have the children get their shirts, cloaks, and belts. Then have kids stand in a circle and say the following prayer. As you say each part of the prayer, have children put on the piece of clothing you mention, and offer assistance if needed.

Dear God,

Thank you for giving us everything we need to live, including clothes!

Just like we put on our *tunics,* help us put on kindness and be kind like

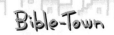

Bible-Town Tip

Grocery stores usually have small gingerbread men. If you can't find these, you can modify the snack by giving each child a plain round cookie with two chocolate chips for eyes. Arms and legs can be made with pretzel sticks attached with dabs of frosting or cream cheese. Kids can make the clothing similar to the way they would for the gingerbread men.

Jesus was. Pause for the children to put on their shirts.

Just like we put on our *belts*, help us put on caring like Jesus was caring. Pause for the children to put on their belts.

Just like we put on our *cloaks*, help us put on love for everyone, just like Jesus loves everyone. Pause for the children to put on their cloaks.

In Jesus' name, amen.

Additions

• You may wish to let the children put on their Bible-times clothes and walk around any of the components of the Bible town that you've made.

• If you have extra licorice strips, kids can make necklaces by threading round cereal pieces on the licorice. Children can wear the necklaces with their Bible-times clothing.

• Set up a center with dolls. Provide materials that the children can use to dress the dolls in Bible-times clothing. You may want to purchase commercially available dolls that come dressed in clothing from biblical times.

• Have the children each find a partner and take off their partner's shoes. Have them help each other trace their feet on a piece of cardboard using a pencil or marker. It's best if kids trace the shapes fairly close to the actual size of their feet. Then tell the children to write their names on each of their foot shapes. (You will need to help your younger preschoolers do this.) You may also wish to have the children use markers to decorate inside the foot shapes. Have an adult cut out the shapes and use a sharp pencil or pen to poke two holes in the cardboard sandals near the "arch" of the foot. Thread leather or fabric strips through the holes by going down from the top through one hole, underneath to the second hole, and back through to the top. Make sure both sides of the ties are even.

Bible-Town Take-Home Page

head covering

sash

tunic

Today children heard the story of a sick woman who touched Jesus' cloak and was healed (Luke 8:42b-48), and they learned that God wants us to be kind and caring like Jesus. Children also learned about clothing from biblical times.

Your child can make a Bible-times paper doll! Cut out the doll and clothing. If you want to make the doll more durable, cut out the doll and glue it to a piece of thin cardboard. After the glue dries, cut the cardboard around the doll.

Your child may want to put on a puppet show with the new doll to tell others about life in biblical times. To help the doll stand on its own, stick it in a small piece of modeling dough. You can make a puppet stage using a large cereal box. Tape the top of an empty box closed. Cut out around the front panel, leaving about a one-inch margin. Then cut out a door in the back panel. Paint or decorate the stage, then let your child put on a show!

Our Daily Bread

Food in Bible Times

The Foundation

God gives us all that we need.

John 6:1-13

The Background

The feel of supple dough, the smell of fresh-baked loaves, the taste of warm bread with melted butter—our senses naturally draw us to bread. Bread and grains are featured prominently throughout Scripture. The story of Ruth, for example, revolves around grain. Jesus used five loaves of bread and two fish to feed more than five thousand people. The word *bread* is used hundreds of times in the Bible—from unleavened bread to Jesus' calling himself the bread of life. Bread is important for our nutritional needs and symbolic of our spiritual needs.

It's easy to take bread for granted today with a variety of loaves readily available at the store. However in many places around the world, making and baking the daily bread is an important and time-consuming task. For thousands of years, the skills of planting and harvesting the grain, grinding the grain, and making bread would have been learned early in life.

To bake the bread, people used several different methods, two of which the children will learn about in this lesson. The first method used a baking plate over an open fire pit. Dough was shaped into flat cakes that were put on an iron or earthen plate over the fire. When the bread had browned on one side, it was flipped over to cook the other side.

Bread could also be baked inside a rounded earthen oven, which was about two feet high. Loaves would be placed onto a clean surface inside, and a clay top with a stone handle covered the oven. Grass, straw, and leaves were heaped on top of the closed oven, and then set on fire. The heat from the fire would permeate the walls, and the oven became hot enough to cook the bread inside.

This lesson will guide children in discovering the process of bread baking, give them an appreciation for their daily bread, and help them understand that God gives us all that we need.

The Tools

- Bible
- large piece of cardboard
- aluminum foil
- masking tape
- flour
- water
- bowls
- 1 roll of bread per child plus a few extras
- 2 paper fish
- 12 baskets
- newspapers
- red, orange, and yellow tissue paper
- a bag of sticks
- a large bag of twigs, leaves, and grasses (or strips of newspaper)
- large cardboard box with lid
- a variety of bread types including flour tortillas, pita bread, and loaves of bread
- modeling dough or bread dough
- tablecloth
- wheat pita bread
- honey
- napkins
- CD player
- children's music CD

The Excavation

Cut a piece of cardboard into a 2- to 3-foot diameter circle. Cover the circle with foil, and secure the foil with tape. This will represent a metal surface to bake bread over an open fire. To make an enclosed clay oven, use a box with a lid. If you'd like, you can use a cement stepping stone as the floor inside the box "oven."

Put five rolls of bread and two paper fish into one of the baskets and set it aside for later.

The Project

Ribbon-Cutting

For this activity, you can have children wash their hands both before and after they work with the dough.

Tell children to sit in a circle. Ask:

- **Who can tell me what bread is made of?**

- **How do flour, water, and the other ingredients turn into bread?**

Say: **Today you get to make dough. Dough is made by mixing flour, water, and other ingredients. For a long time people have made bread using ingredients similar to the ones we use today.**

Set out large bowls for children to share. Put flour and water in each bowl, and encourage children to work together to mix the dough. Add water or flour to each bowl as needed. Encourage children to roll the dough into balls then flatten the balls into flat loaves. Ask:

- **What would happen if we cooked this dough?**

- **Where does your family usually get bread?**

Say: **Sometimes our families bake dough to make bread. Sometimes we buy bread from the store. It worked the same way in Bible times. Most people made bread at home, but sometimes they bought bread from others who made it. God gave people what they needed to make or buy food in Bible times, and God gives us what we need to get our food today.**

Whistle While You Work

Teach children this active song to the tune of "The Mulberry Bush." Kids can also sing the song at the end of the "Framework" activity.

Sing

This is the way we mix the dough, mix the dough, mix the dough.
   (Pretend to mix dough with your fingers.)
This is the way we mix the dough.
God gives us what we need.

This is the way we knead the dough, knead the dough, knead the dough.
   (Use both hands to push down as if you're playing with modeling dough.)
This is the way we knead the dough.
God gives us what we need.

This is the way we bake the bread, bake the bread, bake the bread.
> *(Place one hand on top of the other, as if putting dough on a flat surface.)*

This is the way we bake the bread.

God gives us what we need.

This is the way we eat the bread, eat the bread, eat the bread. *(Pretend to eat a piece of bread and rub your tummy.)*

This is the way we eat the bread.

God gives us what we need.

Blueprint

Have kids sit on the floor, and open your Bible to John 6:1-13.

Say: **Today we're going to hear a wonderful story about Jesus doing a miracle with food. Food is one of my favorite subjects. Some of my favorite foods are** [name some favorite foods]. Ask:

- **What are your favorite foods?**

- **Have you ever had a picnic lunch in the park?**

- **Have you ever had to share a picnic lunch with everyone at the park? What do you think that would be like?**

Say: **That would be an unusual situation! Well our story today is un-usual, but it's also true. Jesus was teaching people about God. He talked for a long time, and the people became very hungry.** Ask:

- **Where would you go if you were hungry and wanted some food?**

Say: **These people were far away from any place to get food. Lots of people were listening to Jesus. It says in the Bible that there were five thou-sand men, and that doesn't include all the women and children who were there. That's as many people as there are in some small towns. "Wow, that's a lot of people!" Say that with me.** Lead the children in saying the words and stretching their arms open wide.

Not only was that a lot of people, but in that crowd only one person had brought something to eat. A young boy had five loaves of bread and two fish. Hold up your basket of five rolls and two paper fish. **I need someone to pretend to be the boy with the food.** Give the basket to a child, and have the child stand in front with you. Ask:

- **Would the food in the basket be enough to feed all the people in a small town?**

- **What would you do if you had to feed so many people?**

Say: **Well Jesus had a great plan. He wanted to do a miracle for all the people.** Ask:

- **What is a miracle?**

- **Who can make miracles happen?**

Say: **Only God can do miraculous things. So Jesus prayed and thanked God. Then an amazing miracle occurred, and those few loaves of bread and two fish became enough food to feed the whole crowd.** Ask:

- **How do you think that could happen?**

Say: **It's hard to imagine what that must have looked like, so let's act it out.** Ask for another volunteer. Have the first child give the basket of food to the second child. Tell kids to close their eyes and bow their heads as the second child prays, "Thank you, God, for the food." While kids have their eyes closed, put enough rolls into the basket for everyone to have one. Then have children open their eyes.

Say: **I put this bread in the basket. But when Jesus prayed, a miracle occurred and there was more food than the people could eat. Now we'll pass the basket around, and everyone can take a roll—but don't eat it yet. What's amazing is that all the people in the crowd got to eat until their tummies were really full.** Ask:

- **If your dad was in the crowd, how much food do you think he could eat?**

- **How much food do you think *five thousand* dads could eat?**

Say: **What's even more amazing is that after all the people had eaten until they were full, there was still food left.** Ask:

- **How much leftover food do you think they had?**

Get out all of the baskets and say: **If you think there were three baskets of leftovers, stand up and take three little bites of your bread.** Let three children hold three of the baskets. **OK. Now if you think that there were six baskets of leftovers, stand up and eat six little bites of your roll.** Give three more baskets to three more children. **If you think there were nine baskets of leftovers, stand up and eat nine tiny bites of your roll.** Pass out baskets to three more children. **In the Bible it says that Jesus asked his disciples to gather the leftovers, and they came back with twelve full baskets.** Give the last three baskets to the children. Ask:

- **How much food did Jesus start with?**

- **If Jesus only had a few loaves of bread and two fish to start with, but all these baskets were full after everyone ate, where do you think all of that food came from?**

Bible-Town Tip

If you have fewer than twelve children in your class, give each child more than one basket, or put some of the baskets on the floor in front of the children.

• How does that make you feel about Jesus?

Say: **Learning about our wonderful Jesus makes me want to rejoice. Let's jump and say, "Jesus is amazing!"** Ask:

• What else can we say to tell Jesus how much we love him?

Jump and say the things the children suggest.

Say: **All this talk about bread makes me wonder just how bread was made during Bible times. Let's learn about how people made bread when Jesus lived.**

Framework

Ask:

• Have you or your mom and dad ever cooked foods over a campfire or in a fireplace?

• What kinds of foods did you cook over the fire?

Say: **Campfire food always tastes *so* good. Let's pretend to cook bread over a fire just like people did in Jesus' time. First we need to make the campfire that we'll use to bake the bread.**

Show the children how to make stones out of newspaper and masking tape. Give each child a large sheet or two of newspaper. Have kids loosely crumple up the paper into balls. Use the masking tape to hold the paper rocks together. Place the stones in a circle to form an open fire pit. In the center of the stones, let the children arrange sticks and red, orange, and yellow tissue paper to simulate a fire.

Hold up the foil-covered cardboard circle and say: **We're going to use this circle as a metal plate to cook our bread. What a fantastic job you've done in making this campfire. Now I'll place this metal plate on the rocks over the fire.** Ask:

• What do you do to keep yourself safe if you're cooking over a fire?

• What kinds of breads could we cook over a fire like this?

Hold up a tortilla. Say: **This is similar to the bread we could bake on this metal plate. The baker would put the bread on the top of the metal. When the bread was golden brown on one side, the baker would quickly flip it over.** Demonstrate this using the tortilla. Let the children each have a chance to put a tortilla on the "cooking plate" and then pick up the tortilla and flip it over. Then put the tortillas in one of the baskets.

Say: **Making bread over an open fire was not the only way to make bread. People could also bake bread in an oven, but the ovens in Bible times were very different from the ones we have today.** Hold the box with a lid and say: **The ovens were actually a rounded shape made from clay, but we'll use this box as our oven.** Take the lid off the box and set it aside. **After I have made some nice bread dough and shaped it into a loaf, I can set it on the clean floor of the oven.** Put a loaf of bread inside the box.

Often a group of people shared the oven, and many loaves would fit inside. Once the bread was placed inside, the lid was put on top. Then people would heap grass, straw, and leaves all over the outside, and set it on fire. The fire made the clay walls get so hot that the bread would bake inside the oven. Let's pretend to do that. Put the lid on the box. Have the kids set the twigs, leaves, and grasses (or newspaper strips) over and all around the box.

After all the things outside the oven had burned up and the oven had baked for a while, the people would let the oven cool and then open it up. Have the children collect all the plant materials, put them into the bag, and set the bag aside. Take the lid off and bring out the loaf of bread. Then ask:

- **How is this kind of oven different or the same as your oven at home?**

- **How would you feel if you had to share your oven with many neighbors?**

Let the children pretend to bake bread at both cooking sites using several different types of bread. You can also let kids form loaves using modeling dough or real bread dough.

Builders Banquet

Have kids wash their hands before this activity. Spread a woven mat or tablecloth on the floor. Set out napkins, and have the children sit around the edges of the tablecloth. Serve wheat pita bread with honey.

Say: **In Jesus' day it was common to say a prayer of thanksgiving before and after the meal. Let's bow our heads and close our eyes as I say this prayer: Blessed are you, O Lord God, who brings bread out of the earth. In Jesus' name, amen.**

Let the children drizzle some honey onto the pita bread and enjoy their treats. While the kids are eating, ask:

- **At home what do you pray before you eat a meal?**

- **How do you think God might feel when he hears your prayers?**

- **What do you do at the end of a meal at home?**

When the children have finished with their snacks, say: **Let's take a moment to say a prayer at the end of our meal: Blessed are you, O Lord God, who brings bread out of the earth. In Jesus' name, amen.**

Dedication

Set up a CD player with a CD of children's music. Have the children sit in a circle. Say: *Jehovah-jireh* **means "God the provider." Say that with me: "Jehovah-jireh means God the provider." When we thank God for our food, we are thanking him for giving us all we need.**

Let's play a game like Hot Potato, but we're going to use a bread roll instead. I'll play some music while you pass the roll around the circle. When I stop the music, the person holding the bread can say, "Thank you, God." Begin the game, and stop the music at various times as kids pass the bread around the circle.

Additions

• Set up an area where the children can scoop, measure, pour, and mix the following dry ingredients: red or brown lentils, raw almonds, wheat grains, barley, and various types of dried beans.

• Provide modeling dough and small bread pans, and let children pretend to make loaves of bread.

• Set out old magazines, scissors, glue sticks, and paper for the children to make collages of other foods that God gives them.

Bible-Town Take-Home Page

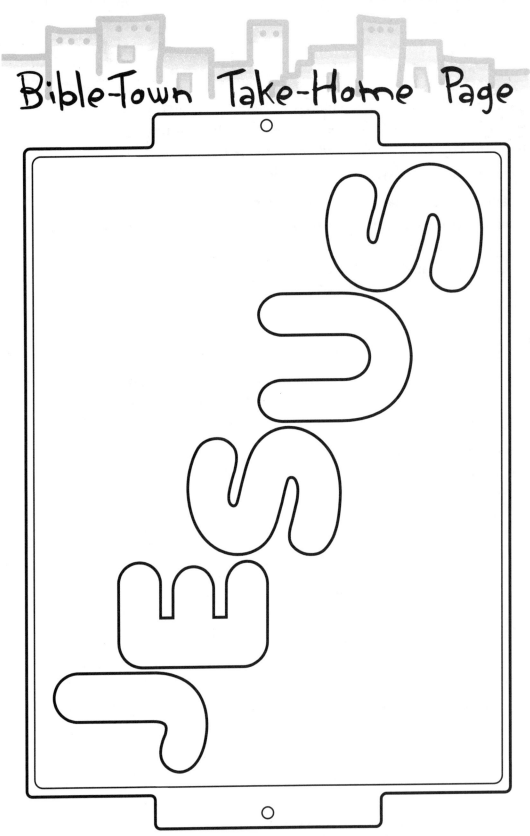

Today kids heard the story of Jesus feeding the five thousand (John 6:1-13), and they learned that God gives us all that we need. Children also learned how bread was made in biblical times.

Have fun making some bread at home. Buy a hot roll mix and follow the simple directions. Form rolls into letters to spell J-E-S-U-S. Remind your child of the verse in which Jesus calls himself the bread of life (John 6:35).

While grocery shopping, take a moment to count how many different kinds of bread are available. Select a type of bread that your family hasn't tried before. Bring the bread home and eat it while reading the story of Jesus feeding the five thousand.

Reading and Writing

Schooling in Bible Times

The Background

Children in biblical times began their education by learning the Scriptures at home. After the age of about six, the boys attended school at the local synagogue. Young girls typically continued their education at home. By the time a boy was thirteen, he was considered a young man and was expected to be able to recite from memory all the verses used in the services. Only a few Jewish boys continued to study with a rabbi when they grew older. The goal of higher education was to help the student become an expert in the Old Testament.

Synagogue classes were held inside the synagogue, in an attached room, or outside in the open air. There were no desks or chairs. To do their lessons, students either stood, sat on the ground, or worked from wooden benches facing the teacher. They wrote on clay or wax-covered tablets using a wooden stylus. The Hebrew alphabet was memorized along with many portions of Scripture. Students also learned arithmetic and religious rituals. Until age ten, boys were taught to read and write from the Old Testament. From age ten to fifteen, students learned the traditional law as the main subject. Students over fifteen years old took part in theological discussions.

The synagogue school was conducted by the hazzan. The hazzan was in charge of the sacred scrolls during public worship. He also recited prayers and blessings and would announce the beginning of the Sabbath by sounding the shofar (ram's horn) three times from the synagogue roof.

Synagogues were usually built of stone. They contained articles of furniture such as a chest or cabinet containing scrolls wrapped in linen, an elevated platform which included a type of podium or reading desk, lamps and candelabra, and benches for sitting. The focal point was the cabinet that contained the Torah (or the Law) and other sacred scrolls.

The Foundation

God wants us to learn about him.

Luke 2:41-52

In this lesson, kids will discover that God wants us to learn about him.

The Tools

- Bible
- overhead projector
- transparency of "The Synagogue" (p. 39)
- 4 or more stand-up playhouse figures
- modeling dough
- craft sticks
- copies of "Hebrew Alphabet" (p. 38)
- plastic foam cups, 1 for each child
- cotton swabs
- fine-tip markers of various colors including red and yellow
- gel pens
- roll of wrapping paper
- empty wrapping paper tube
- carpet squares, 1 for each child
- bricks and boards
- lace tablecloth or pieces of fabric
- pretzel sticks
- crackers
- cream cheese
- plastic knife
- napkins

The Excavation

Copy the picture of "The Synagogue" (p. 39) onto an overhead transparency. Set up an overhead projector on a table near a wall. Focus the image so that the synagogue is proportionate to the playhouse figures you are using, and set up a table against the wall under the image.

Make several photocopies of the "Hebrew Alphabet" handout (p. 38).

The Project

Ribbon-Cutting

Have children sit in a circle, then ask:

- **How many of you go to school? What is that like?**

- **Do you have brothers or sisters who go to school?**

Say: **When Jesus was a young boy, he went to school too. His school was in a building called a synagogue, which is like a church. Children in the church school would learn the alphabet, just like some of you are learning. But instead of writing on paper, the children wrote on clay tablets. They wrote using a small pointed rod called a stylus, which looked kind of like a pencil.**

Give each child some modeling dough. Direct children to spread the dough on a table in the shape of a rectangular tablet. Then give each child a craft stick, and let the kids practice drawing and erasing their work in the dough.

Say: **The children practiced reading words in the Bible, and then they wrote the verses on their tablets. While the children learned to write, they were also learning about God. The words they read were in a different language than ours. They learned to spell using twenty-two Hebrew letters.**

Show the children a copy of the Hebrew text and alphabet from page 38. Tell them that the Hebrew words say, "Hear, O Israel! The Lord is our God, the Lord alone." Compare the Hebrew writing with the English translation. Tell the children that Hebrew is read from right to left and that the dots and dashes above and below the letters aid in pronunciation. Set out several copies of the "Hebrew Alphabet" handout, and let kids practice writing one or two of the simpler letters. Ask:

- **What words can you write?**

- **Where did you learn to write?**

Bible-Town Tip

You might want to have children make their own "clay tablets" by directing them to spread the modeling dough over cardboard or on sturdy plastic plates.

Whistle While You Work

Teach kids this simple song to the tune of "The Mulberry Bush."

Sing

This is the way we walk to school,
Walk to school, walk to school.
This is the way we walk to school,
Just like Jesus did.

This is the way we learn to write,
Learn to write, learn to write.
This is the way we learn to write,
Just like Jesus did.

Blueprint

Have kids sit in a circle.

Say: **Many children look forward to their first day of school.** Ask:

- **How do you feel when you think about going to school?**

- **What do you suppose Jesus thought about on his first day of school?**

Say: **Like other children in Bible times, Jesus was taught at home by his parents until he was about six years old. Then he went to school at the synagogue, which is like a church. There, with other Jewish boys, he studied verses from the Bible to help him learn to read and write. Girls in Bible times did not go to the synagogue school but were taught at home by their moms.**

Many things are different today from what they were like when Jesus went to school. There were no cars or buses to take children to school. Jesus would have walked to the church school, or synagogue, to do his lessons. Let's pretend that it's the first day of school and we're waking up to get ready to go to school.

Have children lie down or put their heads down on a table, and dim the lights in the classroom. "Wake" the children as you turn the lights on. Have children pretend to get dressed, eat their breakfast, gather their school supplies, and walk through town to school. As kids pretend to walk to school, have them sing a verse of the song they learned earlier.

Create a tabletop synagogue by focusing the overhead transparency onto a nearby wall. Use small, free-standing playhouse figures as Mary, Joseph, Jesus, and other people. Let the kids take turns arranging the figures on the table so that the shadows are positioned in the synagogue. Then have children sit down together. Open your Bible to Luke 2:41-52, and tell kids that today's story is in God's Word.

Say: **Jesus loved to learn about God. He probably spent many hours at the synagogue school talking with the teachers, who were called rabbis. He asked them questions and listened carefully to their answers. Then he asked them more questions. Sometimes Jesus asked them questions that were hard to answer.** Have one or more children arrange figures on the tabletop to represent Jesus with the teachers. Have them place figures to represent Mary and Joseph nearby.

When Jesus was twelve, he traveled with Mary and Joseph for a special celebration in Jerusalem. When it was time to go, Mary and Joseph started home with many other people who had come for the celebration. Have children remove the figures of Mary and Joseph.

After traveling awhile, Mary and Joseph realized that Jesus was not with them. They didn't know where he was. They thought he might be traveling with the other children or walking home with his relatives or friends. Mary and Joseph became worried and set out looking for Jesus. They hurried back to Jerusalem and looked all through the town. Finally they found him! Have children place the figures for Mary and Joseph back on the table.

And do you know what Jesus was doing when Mary and Joseph found him? Jesus was in the Temple, asking the rabbis questions and listening to them teach. When Mary and Joseph asked Jesus why he stayed in the church when it was time to go home, he explained that it was very important for him to be in God's house. Jesus knew that the most important things to learn were the things about God.

Turn off the overhead projector. Tell kids that it's important that they learn to read and write and learn about the world they live in. But it's even more important for them to learn about God. Ask:

• How do you feel when you go to church?

• How do you think Jesus felt when he was talking with the teachers?

• Why do you think Jesus was happy to be at the church?

• What are some things you have learned about God?

Framework

Invite the children to help make their own church school and pretend to be in school with Jesus.

Say: **Let's make our own church school like the one Jesus might have gone to. First we'll need to set up candles inside the church school. The light helped the students see to do their work, and it also reminded them of God who helped them learn and understand his Word. Let's pretend to light the candles before we do our schoolwork.**

Give each child a plastic foam cup and half of a cotton swab. Instruct children to color the cotton swabs with red and yellow markers. Then have children each turn their foam cup upside down and poke the cotton swab through the bottom of the cup so that the end of the swab rests on the cup (see illustration).

Say: **People in Bible times did not have books like we have today.** Hold up a Bible. **In Jesus' time, Bible verses were written on long strips of special paper, called parchment. When the parchment was rolled onto a rod, it was called a scroll. Let's make a very large scroll that all of you can write on.**

Attach the free end of a roll of wrapping paper to an empty wrapping paper

tube. Then unroll the paper, and let kids use gel pens or fine-tip markers to write letters or draw on the plain white side of the paper.

Your class can build two brick-and-board shelves by alternating planks and bricks. When kids have finished, cover the shelves with a lace tablecloth or fabric, and place the scroll on the shelves. Then give each child a carpet square to sit on.

Say: **Let's think about what Jesus might have done as a young boy. In the church school he spent time learning lessons from the Bible. He listened carefully to what his teachers said. He was quick to help and always ready to learn. Let's pretend that we're going to school like Jesus did.**

Children can take turns being the teacher and leading the other students with handwriting practice on their clay tablets, singing, or memorizing a Bible verse such as, "I love you, O Lord" (from Psalm 18:1). Ask:

- **What do you like about this kind of church school?**
- **What do you like best about your church?**

Builders Banquet

This is a time when children have permission to play with their food! Before you begin, have children wash their hands. Help children use plastic knives to spread cream cheese on crackers, then let your kids use pretzel sticks to draw in the cream cheese. They can write Hebrew letters, the first letter of their name, or follow the rhyme below as you show them how to make some simple letters. Emphasize the letter sound as you read the rhyme. Then, before the children eat their snacks, take a moment to pray.

Learn starts with a little "l,"
Straight up and down.
We learn about God
In our Wee-Built Bible Town.

"T" is like a little "l,"
But at the top there's a line.
God teaches us truth
One day at a time.

"I" is like a little "l,"
Put a dot at the top.
I love to hear about God
And I learn a lot.

Dedication

Arrange the carpet squares in a circle and ask the children to sit down.

Say: **God wants us to learn all about the wonderful world he has created. He wants us to learn how to read, how to write, how to add, and how to subtract. But most of all, God wants us to learn about him. When we learn, we use our eyes to watch, our ears to listen, our hands and bodies to explore, and our mouths to ask important questions. That's what Jesus did when he was a young boy. Let's play a game to see if you can be like Jesus.**

Ask the children to pretend to be Jesus when he was little. Tell them that you will ask them a question, and they can pretend to do what they think Jesus would have done.

It's early in the morning
Almost time to go to school.
Mother says, "Wake up and stretch."
What would Jesus do? *(Open eyes wide, yawn, and stretch.)*

It's time to hurry off to school,
Put on your cap and shoes.
Father says, "It's time to go."
What would Jesus do? *(Pretend to put on shoes and cap.)*

The children in the church school
Hear lessons old and new.
The rabbi says, "Let's bow and pray."
What would Jesus do? *(Bow head, fold hands in prayer.)*

The Bible is God's Word,
It tells of God's love for you.
God says, "Open up my book."
What would Jesus do? *(Place hands together to form a book.)*

Say: **Let's thank God together.** Have kids say this prayer with you.

Dear Lord,

Thank you for my church where I can come to hear your Word and learn about you.

In Jesus' name, amen.

Additions

• Before class, form thick cotton string into the shape of a Hebrew letter, and glue it onto a 2x4-inch wooden block. Make several of these blocks. After the glue has dried, spread out a long piece of white shelf paper. (Do not remove the backing.) Paint the strings with water-based paint, and let the children use the printing blocks like rubber stamps to fill the paper with Hebrew letters. Attach the paper to two rolling pins, and put it with the scroll the kids made earlier.

• Set out modeling dough. Let kids each take a large piece of dough (about fist-sized) and flatten it. Have kids roll the left and right sides toward the middle, leaving enough space in the center to look like an opened scroll. Then let children use craft sticks to make letters in the dough.

• Follow your favorite recipe and make sugar cookie dough. Let kids roll the dough into "snakes." Shape the snakes into Hebrew letters or other letters and numbers. Then bake the cookies and let the children enjoy the tasty treats.

Bible-Town Take-Home Page

Today kids heard the story of Jesus as a boy at the Temple in Jerusalem (Luke 2:41-52), and they discovered that it's important to learn about God. Children also learned about schooling in biblical times.

Help your child cut yarn scraps and glue them onto the outline of the Hebrew letter. Allow the glue to dry. (If you don't have yarn scraps handy, your child can use crayons or markers to color in the letter.) Then give your child two cardboard bathroom tissue rolls. Glue or tape each end of the scroll to the tissue rolls. Then roll up the scroll from right to left, and let your child use a ribbon or yarn to tie the scroll. Your child can paint, color, or decorate a paper lunch sack with brightly colored paper and store the scroll inside. The scroll can remind your child that God wants us to learn about him.

Alef

Hebrew Alphabet

ט	ח	ז	ו	ה	ד	ג	ב	א
Tet	Chet	Zayin	Vav	He	Dalet	Gimel	Bet	Alef
(T)	(Ch)	(Z)	(V/O/U)	(H)	(D)	(G)	(B/V)	(Silent)

ס	ן	נ	ם	מ	ל	כ	כ	י
Samech	Nun	Nun	Mem	Mem	Lamed	Khaf	Kaf	Yod
(S)	(N)	(N)	(M)	(M)	(L)	(Kh)	(K/Kh)	(Y)

ת	ש	ר	ק	ץ	צ	ף	פ	ע
Tav	Shin	Resh	Qof	Tzade	Tzade	Fe	Pe	Ayin
(T/S)	(Sh/S)	(R)	(Q)	(Tz)	(Tz)	(F)	(P/F)	(Silent)

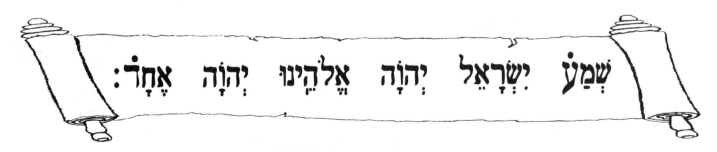

שְׁמַע יִשְׂרָאֵל יְהוָה אֱלֹהֵינוּ יְהוָה אֶחָד:

"Hear, O Israel! The Lord is our God, the Lord alone" (Deuteronomy 6:4).

The Synagogue

Let's Go Fishing!

Occupations in Bible Times

The Background

This lesson will describe three of the jobs mentioned in the Bible (a shepherd, a carpenter, and a fisherman), focusing on the job of a fisherman.

A shepherd's job was an important one because sheep were used for so many things. Sheep were used for food, and the wool and skin were used for clothing. Shepherds needed to be strong, devoted, and selfless because their job was not an easy one. A shepherd had to find food and water for his sheep; protect his flock from predators, robbers, and bad weather; care for injured animals; and retrieve stray sheep. Sometimes shepherds used dogs to help with the sheep. An experienced shepherd knew each of his animals, and the sheep recognized the shepherd's voice. In John 10:1-18, the Bible talks about some of the skills required to be a shepherd. Jesus describes himself in this passage as the Good Shepherd who will give his life for his sheep.

In biblical times, carpenters typically made farm tools, as well as furniture, doors, and roof beams for houses. The word *carpenter* could also be used to mean a craftsman or builder. Jesus is described in Mark 6:3 as a carpenter and in Matthew 13:55 as a carpenter's son. In biblical times, a son was likely to learn an occupation from his father. The son would be the apprentice, and the father would be the expert or teacher. Most craft workers learned their skills as children, and by the age of about fifteen, they would know enough to set up in a business of their own. Jesus probably helped his father in his carpenter's workshop.

In Jesus' time, a carpenter was considered to have a common, ordinary job that didn't require any formal education; people who were well-educated would not choose to be a carpenter. Being a carpenter was not the type of profession a king would have—that's why some people were surprised by how much Jesus knew, considering that he probably hadn't had much formal education.

When we think of fishing today, we think of it as a fun way to spend a day. But in biblical times, fishing was a tough job. In fact, the Bible does not mention fishing as recreation. A fisherman might use a spear or harpoon, a hook, or a net. On the Sea of Galilee, the fishermen used small boats with oars and perhaps sails, and they often fished at night. If a net was used, the fish could be dragged to shore or emptied into the boat. Read about Jesus and the miraculous catch of fish in John 21:1-14. This passage is a great illustration of fishing in biblical times.

It's interesting to note that Jesus called his disciples out of a number of occupations—from fishermen to tax collectors. In this lesson, children will learn that God wants us to tell others about Jesus.

The Tools

- Bible
- 2 cinder blocks
- fabric or brown paper
- packing tape
- large cardboard box, such as a diaper box
- utility knife
- wooden dowel approximately 3 feet long or a cardboard wrapping paper tube
- white paper or fabric
- blue painters tape or masking tape
- a skein of wool, a wool scarf, or a pile of raw wool
- a sheet (or a net)
- newspapers
- brown markers
- rope
- saltines
- tuna salad
- napkins
- paper cups
- lemon-lime soda
- blue food coloring

The Excavation

Cover the cinder blocks with fabric or brown paper so that they aren't scratchy; use clear packing tape to hold the fabric or paper in place.

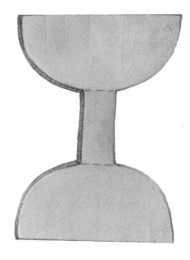

Cut a half-circle out of one side of a large box with the curve touching the bottom edge of the box. Repeat this cut on the other side of the box to make two half-circles that are connected by the bottom of the box.

Take a dowel or wrapping paper tube and tape a triangular piece of white paper or fabric to it to form the sail.

Using the blue painters tape or masking tape, make a circle on the floor where your lake will be. Make sure it is big enough for the cardboard boat.

The Project

Ribbon-Cutting

Have the children sit in a circle on the floor.

Say: **We're going to play a game. When I point to you, stand up and act out what you'd like to be when you grow up. The rest of us will try to guess what you're doing. So if you want to be a firefighter, you could pretend to be putting out a fire with water from a hose. If you want to be a doctor, you could pretend to give someone a shot or listen to someone's heart.**

Point to each child in the circle, and let everyone have a turn. Help children think of actions if they're not sure what to do. Tell kids that all of these things they can do when they grow up are called jobs. Ask:

• **What are some other jobs you know about?**

Say: **A job is something you do to earn money. Back in Bible times, people had jobs, too. We're going to learn about some of those jobs, and find out what God's main job for us is.**

Whistle While You Work

Teach children this song to the tune of "Frère Jacques." You might want to sing this song while you are building the cardboard boat later on.

Sing

Let's go fishing, let's go fishing.
Grab the net, grab the bait!
We're not catching fishies,
But we're telling people
About God. God is great!

Blueprint

As the children sit on the floor in a circle, pass around a skein of wool, a wool scarf, or a pile of raw wool. Ask the children to guess what they are touching. After kids have had a chance to guess, say: **This is wool, which is the fuzzy hair on sheep. A person who takes care of sheep is called a shepherd. In Bible times, being a shepherd was a very important job.** Ask:

• **What things do you think a shepherd would need to do?**

Say: **Shepherds had to find grass and water for their sheep, find any lost sheep, and scare away other animals who might like to eat the sheep.**

You may want to have kids role-play. You can pretend to be the shepherd and the children can be the sheep. Act out situations such as a wolf coming near, a sheep straying, or the shepherd searching for grass and water.

Say: **Some people in Bible times also had jobs as carpenters. In fact, Jesus was a carpenter.** Ask:

• **What do you think a carpenter does?**

Say: **A carpenter is someone who works with wood.** Ask:

• **Would you like to be a carpenter when you grow up?**

• **Do any of your moms or dads make things out of wood?**

Say: **In Bible times, children would work with their dads to learn a skill like working with wood, and when the children were teenagers they would set up their own business.**

Ask the children to get out their "hammers" by making a fist with one hand. Have them pound on "wood" (their other hand) while you say this rhyme:

Jesus was a carpenter, yes sirree!
He came to save us, you and me!

Say: **The last job from Bible times that we're going to learn about is being a fisherman.** Ask:

• **Has anyone ever been fishing?**

• **What did you like about fishing?**

Say: **In Bible times, fishing was a very hard job. Fishermen went out in boats and used nets to catch fish instead of using fishing poles to catch fish like many of us do today.**

Open your Bible and read Matthew 4:18-20 from an easy-to-understand Bible translation.

Say: **Jesus understood that fishing was an important job, but he knew that telling other people about God was an even more important job. Peter and Andrew followed Jesus and told other people about him.**

Take a couple of minutes to have kids pretend to go fishing. Ask the children to get out their make-believe fishing poles.

Say: **When we go fishing nowadays, we usually use a fishing pole to catch fish.**

Explain that people can only catch one fish at a time when they use fishing poles. Next role-play fishing in Bible times. Use a sheet (or a net if you have one), and ask the children to help you cast the net into a make-believe lake. Do this several times until everyone has had a turn to help with the net.

Say: **In Bible times when people went fishing, they could catch lots of fish each time they cast their nets. When Jesus said that Peter and Andrew would be "fishers of men," he meant that they should tell other people about him and how he died for us. So, when we are fishers of men, that means that we should tell *lots* of people about Jesus and his love so that we can do our most important job really well!**

Framework

Start your construction project by putting sheets of newspaper on the floor. Lay the cut box on the newspaper, and have the kids draw lines with brown markers to simulate wood planks on both sides of the boat. (If time and weather permit, you may wish to use brown tempera paint instead—this would be a great outdoor project.)

Next hand each child a strip of blue painters tape or masking tape, and ask kids to make "waves" inside of the lake circle you made earlier. Depending on your class size, you may need more than one roll. If you use masking tape, explain to the children that the waves will be stormy white waves!

Finally, flip the boat over so that the "wooden planks" are face down. Put the two covered cinder blocks close together in the center. Now fold up the boat-shaped ends and secure them with rope by poking a hole on each side of the top of the boat near one end. Leave the other side open for the children to walk in and out of the boat. Then put the dowel or cardboard tube with the sail between the cinder blocks to form a mast.

Remind kids that the disciples were called to be fishers of men and to tell others about Jesus—God wants us to tell others about Jesus too.

Builders Banquet

Enjoy a picnic by your new lake! Have kids wash their hands before this activity. Then have the kids sit around the edge of the lake and let one child thank God for the snacks. Pass out napkins and saltines with tuna salad, and let kids enjoy eating the food. Wash the snacks down with "lake liquid"—lemon-lime soda with a blue food coloring mixed in. Talk about different ways we can tell people about Jesus. Thank God for giving the children such a great job of telling others about Jesus.

Dedication

Let children take turns sitting in the boat pretending to be fishing, then encourage the kids to take turns pretending to be Jesus calling his disciples. Have the child playing Jesus say, "Come, follow me. I will make you fishers of men." This repetition is a great way to help kids remember the Bible passage!

After everyone has had a turn calling the disciples, take a minute to say this prayer:

Dear God,

Thank you for giving us jobs to do. Help us to remember that the most important job we have is telling other people about Jesus.

In Jesus' name, amen.

Additions

• Get an instant-print camera and have the kids sit or stand in the boat. Take a picture for each child to take home. On the bottom of the photo write, "I will make you fishers of men" (Matthew 4:19).

• Make a book about the children's jobs. Give each child three sheets of paper. Ask what jobs or chores the children have to do at home. Examples might include setting the table, picking up toys, or taking care of pets. Help the children write one chore on each page. Next, ask the children to illustrate each chore with a picture. Finally, give each child one more piece of paper. On the bottom write, "My most important job is telling others about Jesus!" For each child, fold a piece of 11x17-inch construction paper in half, and slip the drawings inside. Staple the left edge. If you took instant-print photos, you may wish to glue the photo on each child's cover and title the book "[Child's name]'s Jobs."

• Bring in large stones to put near your "lake." The kids can help place the rocks on the shoreline.

• You may be able to find an inexpensive net at a craft store or party supply store to enhance your lake display. Try looking in the Hawaiian-theme section of the store.

• You can also bring in plastic fish to put in the net, or you can have the children cut out and color paper fish. If you want to have somewhat more realistic fish, cut two pieces of paper into the shape of fish, then tape or staple the edges together, leaving a small opening. Make several fish, and ask the children to color the fish. When kids have finished, stuff the fish with newspaper or paper scraps, and staple or tape closed the last part of the edge.

Bible-Town Take-Home Page

Jesus

Peter

Andrew

In today's lesson, kids heard about the calling of Jesus' first disciples (Matthew 4:18-20), and they learned that God wants us to tell others about Jesus. Children also learned about the occupations of a carpenter, a shepherd, and a fisherman.

Remind your child of the Bible story with this fun activity. Cut a sheet of blue construction paper to make a lake. Then let your child glue a small cardboard container onto the lake to represent a boat. (A cardboard hot dog holder would work well; grocery store delis often have these thin "boats.")

Make a sail by attaching a piece of construction paper to a straw or craft stick. Put the end of the straw into a small bit of clay to help the sail stand up in the boat.

For added fun, you can make a net from fabric netting or from plastic netting (like the netting around fruit in a grocery store). Cut out fish from paper or use a shaped paper punch to make small fish, and glue these onto the net. You might also want to glue a piece of paper onto the lake that says, "I will make you fishers of men" (Matthew 4:19).

Then cut out the figures of Jesus and the disciples, and use them to act out the story of Jesus calling the disciples.

Treasure at the Marketplace

Shopping in Bible Times

The Foundation

God wants us to treasure Jesus more than anything.

Matthew 2:1-11

The Background

Bleating sheep, clucking chickens, colorful fabrics, leather sandals, sweet-smelling melons—not to mention the chatter of people bartering and the laughter of children playing. These were the sights and sounds of the marketplace. Israel had trade connections with many parts of the Roman Empire and beyond. The people of Israel undoubtedly encountered a variety of wares in the markets, and they certainly encountered many different people.

The marketplace functioned as the center of life in biblical times. People brought their sick to the marketplace to be healed by Jesus (Mark 6:56). The unemployed looked for work or handouts, and the Pharisees walked through the marketplace hoping to be seen. Sometimes marketplaces were the stage for trials and philosophical debates.

Markets were often located near the city gates. People would come to buy and sell wares, give speeches, have celebrations, and watch military displays. But probably more than anything else, the people in the marketplace would spend their time talking.

In today's lesson, children will learn about the marketplace in biblical times, and more important, that God wants us to treasure Jesus more than anything.

The Tools

- Bible
- 4 large cardboard boxes
- 4 towels or large pieces of fabric
- fruits and vegetables (real or plastic) in baskets
- candles and candleholders
- yarn, various fabrics, and woven items

- sandals and shoes
- yellow paper star
- large plastic coins, at least 6 for each child
- magazine pictures of things people need
- resealable plastic bags, 1 for each child
- suitcase loosely packed with items for a trip
- 3 wrapped presents to represent gold, incense, and myrrh
- nuts, dried fruits, fresh fruits
- small cups

The Excavation

Set out four cardboard boxes to use as booths later in the lesson, and put a towel or piece of fabric in each one. Then in one box, put fruits and vegetables (real or plastic) in baskets; in the second box, place a variety of candles and candleholders; in the third box, place yarn, fabric, and woven items; and in the fourth box, put sandals and shoes.

Tape a yellow paper star to a wall near the teaching area, or hang it from the ceiling. (Make sure the star is in a place you'll be able to easily reach later.) Then hide the plastic coins around the room. Finally, cut out pictures from magazines showing pictures of things people need, such as houses, clothes, and food.

The Project

Ribbon-Cutting

Have kids form a circle and sit down.

Say: **We all have favorite things, or treasures, that we really like.** Ask:

- **What are some of your favorite treasures at home?**

Say: **You get to hunt for treasure today. I hid some plastic coins around the room to use in our lesson today. As you find the coins, count them. When you have six coins, come sit with me in a circle. If you see friends who are having a hard time finding the coins, help them. It's important that we help one another.**

Give each child a resealable plastic bag, and let the children hunt for the plastic coins that you hid earlier. Make sure all the children have a few coins in their bags at the end of the hunt.

After everyone is finished, say: **Shake the coins in your bag. What a nice sound that makes.** Ask:

- What did you like about hunting for treasure coins?

Say: **These coins are just for fun—they're pretend. They're not real treasure.** Ask:

- What are some things that are more important than these coins?

- What do you think God thinks is important?

Say: **Later you'll use these coins to go shopping at the marketplace that we'll be making today. You'll get to search for treasure. But as we go through our lesson, I want you to be looking for what is the greatest treasure of all.**

Whistle While You Work

Say this lively rhyme to the rhythm of "We're Going on a Bear Hunt." The rhythm of this song is a steady, even pattern of clapping hands together, patting hands on legs, clapping hands together, and patting hands on legs. Have children keep the rhythm, breaking to do the motions in parentheses.

Sing

We're going on a treasure hunt.
We're seeking something special.
What a beautiful day!
We can't wait!

We're coming to some weavers,
Weaving, weaving. *(Pretend to be a weaver.)*
But this is not our treasure.
We'd better move on.

We're coming to some fresh fish,
Fresh fish, fresh fish. *(Pretend to go fishing.)*
But this is not our treasure.
We'd better move on.

We're coming to some carpenters,
Sawing, sawing. *(Pretend to saw wood.)*
But this is not our treasure.
We'd better move on.

We're coming to some grocers,

Melons, fresh bread. (Pretend to eat.)

But this is not our treasure.

We'd better move on.

We're coming to some shepherds.

Baa, baa. Baa, baa. (Act like sheep.)

But this is not our treasure.

We'd better move on.

We're coming to the Temple.

We want to worship Jesus. (Fold hands in prayer.)

We have found our treasure.

Praise God! Praise God!

Blueprint

Open your Bible to Matthew 2:1-11.

Say: **In the Bible, there's a wonderful story about some very special men who were looking for the greatest treasure of all, just like we are. Some people think there were** *three* **men who were searching. Hold up three fingers and wiggle them. Now hold your fingers still. Your fingers look a little like the letter W. This is great because W is the first letter of** *wise men*. **The three men looking for treasure were called wise men. Wiggle your fingers one more time.** Then have kids put their hands down.

The wise men had seen a star in the sky. It might have been like the star here. Point to the star you hung up earlier. **The wise men pointed to the star and wondered, "What does that star mean?" So they got out their scrolls, which were like books, and read about a wonderful king who would be born when this star appeared.** Ask:

• **When they heard the good news about the wonderful new king, how do you think the wise men felt?**

• **How would you feel if you heard about a wonderful king being born?**

Say: **I would be excited, and I'd want to jump for joy! Let's do that together.** Have the children jump up and down a few times and then sit back down.

The three wise men were so excited that they decided to look for this incredible king and give him presents to honor him. What a good idea! Let's pretend to do that, too. Let's pack a suitcase for a trip. Get out the suitcase, and hand out all of the things the children might need to go on the trip.

Then pass the suitcase around, and let the children repack the bag, saying the names of the items as they place them inside.

Display the three wrapped gifts, then say: **Don't forget presents like the wise men took.** Have the children put the gifts in the suitcase. **The wise men went on a long journey searching for a great treasure. They followed the special star. Let's pretend to do that, too.**

Take down the star, and give it to one child. Let another child carry the suitcase. Encourage the children to follow the child with the star around the room. After a minute or two, choose a different child to hold the star and another child to carry the suitcase. If you have time, give all of the children a chance to be the leader with the star. Then hang up the star again, and have kids sit back down.

Say: **Finally the wise men arrived at a city. They may have looked around the marketplace, but couldn't find any signs that said "Treasure King This Way." So they went to the leader of the city to ask if he knew about this treasure of a new king. The ruler said that the king might be found in the little town of Bethlehem. So the wise men left the big city and followed the star to Bethlehem. Their treasure hunt was almost up!** Ask:

• **How do you think the three men felt as they were getting so close to their treasure?**

Say: **Maybe the wise men walked a little faster. We don't know, but they did keep following the star. It led them to the greatest treasure of all! The wonderful king that they'd read about was still just a small child. But that didn't matter. They had found their treasure, and they bowed down to worship King Jesus. Let's bow down too.** Lead the children in bowing. Ask:

• **How do you think the wise men felt when they found their treasure, the baby Jesus?**

• **Who is the greatest treasure of all?**

• **How do you feel now that you've discovered who's the greatest treasure of all?**

Say: **The wise men gave their gifts to King Jesus.** Let three children take the three presents out of the suitcase and put them near the star. **In Bible times, people went to the marketplace to find and to sell treasures. But the wise men didn't find Jesus at the marketplace or even in a palace. Jesus had been born in a stable where animals stayed. When the wise men came to worship Jesus, they brought gold, incense, and myrrh—wonderful gifts that the wise men might have bought in the marketplace. Let's make a marketplace like the one where the wise men may have found the gifts for Jesus.**

Framework

Build a marketplace using the four cardboard boxes. Have the children form four groups, and give each group a box. Tell kids to take the items out of the boxes and turn the boxes over. Then direct the children in each group to drape the towel or piece of fabric over the box as a covering, and let them display the items at the booths. You could also have kids display other items, such as toy fish, containers of spices, toy jewelry, bowls or pots, or toy animals.

Say: **What a great marketplace! You have all done a wonderful job of putting everything together. Let's pretend to be the wise men seeking the baby Jesus.**

Have four children stand at the booths and pretend to be the sellers. Lead the rest of the children in going to each booth and saying, "We have come a long way to find the treasure of a king. Do you know where this treasure is?"

Have each seller respond by saying, "I have this for sale, but I don't know where the special king is." After visiting all the booths, have the children sit down. Ask:

• **How do you think the wise men felt when their treasure—the baby Jesus—was not in the first big city they went to?**

• **After traveling so far, what do you think the wise men might have needed to buy at the marketplace?**

• **What other treasures could they find in the marketplace?**

Say: **You may use the coins you found earlier to buy some needed supplies, or maybe a treasure, at these booths.**

Have the children take turns selling items and shopping. Let kids use their plastic coins to buy items in the marketplace, but remind them to save two coins for the "Builders Banquet" and "Dedication" activities. Ask:

• **What did you like best about shopping at our marketplace?**

• **What did you buy?**

• **Where do you go shopping with your family?**

• **How is shopping nowadays the same or different than it was when Jesus lived?**

Say: **We found some neat treasures in our marketplace. But God doesn't want us to think only of money or gifts. God wants us to treasure Jesus more than anything.**

Builders Banquet

While kids are washing their hands, set out small cups of nuts, dried fruits, and fresh fruits at one of the booths. (Make sure the children don't have food allergies.)

Say: **Here we have some delicious snacks for sale. Each of you may use a coin to buy a snack.**

As children each buy a snack, have them say, "Thank you, Jesus, for being the greatest treasure of all."

Dedication

Have the kids sit in a circle. Make sure each child has one of the plastic coins. Place the magazine pictures of things people need in the center of the circle.

Say: **Look at these pictures of things people need to live.** Ask:

• **What are some of the things you see here?**

Say: **God wants to meet all our needs. He wants us to be warm in the winter with warm clothes and a warm house. He wants us to have food and water so that we can grow healthy and strong. He wants us to have loving families to feel safe and secure.**

But God wants us to treasure Jesus more than anything. We have everything we need to live on earth, but we also have forgiveness through Jesus so that we can be with him in heaven forever. Jesus is the greatest treasure anyone can find!

Isn't God good to give us everything we need? When I think about how good God is to me, I want to thank him. You can thank him, too. You each can buy a picture of something that people need, and we can thank God.

When every child has a picture, say the following prayer: **Thank you, God, for all of these things, and most of all, thank you for Jesus. In Jesus' name, amen.**

Additions

• Invite a guest to come dressed up like a traveler from a faraway land to tell exotic stories about life in other places, as the wise men might have told stories of their travels.

• Set up a table where kids can smell different spices. Talk about the spices from the East, such as cinnamon and curry powder. Ask the children which spices they have tasted before, and explain how the spices are used in cooking.

Bible-Town Take-Home Page

Color all of the items that you need to live each day.

Today kids heard the story of the wise men (Matthew 2:1-11), and they discovered that Jesus is the greatest treasure of all. Children also learned about the market-place in biblical times.

Preschool children are at a perfect age to learn about wise spending. Help them understand the difference be-tween needs and wants. Take a trip to a store, and play a game of I Spy. Go into a store and find an item that people

need. For example, if the item is a coat or sweater, say, "I spy an item used in the winter to keep you warm." Ask your child, "If you didn't have warm clothes for the winter and you had only a little money, what would you need to buy?"

Take notice of all the items that are just extras. Talk about how God is good to provide for all of our needs and how he has given us the greatest treasure in Jesus. Thank God for his great love for us.

Hanging Out at God's House

Worship in Bible Times

The Foundation

God wants us to worship in his house.

Luke 21:37-38

The Background

The Temple in Jesus' day was considered the house of God or the main location where people worshipped God. God's manifest presence dwelt within the walls of the Temple in Jerusalem. Coming into God's presence was one of the highest forms of worship.

The Temple area was surrounded by the Gentiles' Court. This large courtyard was open to Jews and Gentiles alike. Gentiles were prevented from going into the Temple by a low wall called the soreg, and inscriptions warned Gentiles that they risked being put to death if they ventured beyond the wall to enter the Temple.

From the soreg, a series of steps led to the gates of the Temple and into the inner courts. The Women's Court was just inside the Temple walls. This courtyard was an open area surrounded by a balcony. At the far end of the Women's Court, steps led up to the Nicanor Gate. Jewish men and boys were allowed through the gate and into the Israel Court, a long, colonnaded, roofed area. The innermost court, the Priests' Court, surrounded the sanctuary. The altar was in the Priests' Court.

From the Priests' Court, steps led into the sanctuary. Inside the sanctuary were two main areas, the Holy Place and the Holy of Holies. These two areas were separated by a large veil, or curtain, which was torn from top to bottom when Jesus died. Priests performed their regular duties in the Holy Place. But the Holy of Holies could be entered only by the high priest on the Day of Atonement, when he made sacrifices for the sins of the people.

The Temple must have been spectacular as the disciples pointed out its beauty to Jesus. The sanctuary was completed in 18 B.C., although work on some of the other areas continued until A.D. 64. Only six years later, the Romans destroyed the Temple.

In this lesson, children will learn that Jesus taught at the Temple, and they'll discover that God wants us to worship in his house.

The Tools

- Bible
- 4x8-foot sheet of Styrofoam, ½- to ¾-inch thick
- utility knife
- black permanent marker
- strong tape or package of Fun-Tak adhesive
- various worship supplies (such as rhythm instruments and streamers)
- CD player
- CD of children's praise music
- about 15 cardboard blocks (each about the size of a shoe box—or use shoe boxes)
- masking tape
- paper
- graham crackers
- frosting
- string licorice
- plastic knives

The Excavation

Use a utility knife to cut in half the 4x8-foot sheet of Styrofoam. Cut one of the halves in half again. Then cut one of those halves in half. (You should end up with four pieces.) Set aside one of the two smallest pieces. You will use the three remaining pieces to make a temple relief on the wall.

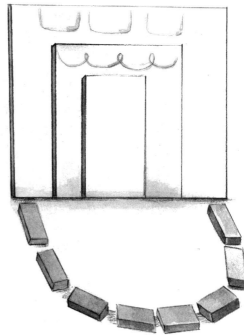

Use tape, or place pieces of Fun-Tak adhesive on the corners and in the center of the back of each piece of foam. Attach the largest piece to the wall first (place it at the bottom of the wall, near the floor). Attach the medium-sized piece to the first piece. Then, attach the smallest piece on top. Be sure there is plenty of space on the floor in front of the attached foam pieces so that children can make a courtyard with blocks later. Use a black marker and decorate the foam to look more like a temple. For example, you might draw two large pillars on each side.

Cut string licorice into 2- to 3-inch pieces, and set these on a table. Also set out frosting, plastic knives, and graham crackers.

The Project

Ribbon-Cutting

Put various worship supplies on the floor. You might include simple rhythm instruments, streamers, and ribbons. Have children sit in a circle around the items. Ask:

- **What kinds of things do we do at church?**

- **Why do we go to church?**

Say: **One of the main reasons we go to church is to worship God.** Ask:

- **What does it mean to worship God?**

Say: **When we worship God, we thank him for all the wonderful things he has done for us. When we worship, we also show God and everybody else how great we think God is. We can worship God anytime or anywhere. But it's really special to worship God together with other people. Let's do that right now.**

Have the children choose from the worship supplies, and encourage children to join in as you sing a song of praise that they are familiar with. Consider using a simple song from a children's praise CD. When children have finished singing, say: **God is here—God is where his people are. God wants to be with us, and he loves your worship. I'm so glad you've come to worship God!**

Whistle While You Work

For another fun song, have kids sing these lyrics to the tune of "Jesus Loves Me," and teach children the motions.

Sing

God's not hiding anywhere! *(Shake head "no.")*
He is here, and he is there. *(Point to floor, and point elsewhere in the room.)*
God sees you, and God sees me. *(Shade eyes and look around.)*
Worship God and you will see! *(Point up to heaven.)*
Yes, my God loves me! *(Place hands on heart.)*
Yes, my God loves me! *(Place hands on heart.)*
Yes, my God loves me! *(Place hands on heart.)*
I love to worship God! *(Raise hands up over head.)*

Blueprint

Have kids sit in a circle.

Say: **Jesus loved to be in God's house.** Ask:

- **What is God's house called?**

- **What do you like about God's house?**

Say: **In Bible times, God's house was called the Temple.** Ask:

- **Why do you think Jesus loved God's house?**

Say: **Jesus went to the Temple to teach people about God. And Jesus prayed when he was in the Temple. Let's pray to God right now. Let's each thank God for one thing he has done for us or given us.** Give each child an opportunity to give a prayer of thanks.

Open your Bible to Luke 21:37-38, and show the children that today's story is in God's Word. Lead the children to an open area of the room, and encourage the kids to participate in this story about Jesus at the Temple. Have the children repeat your words and actions as you tell the story.

Early each day *(stretch and yawn),*
People got out of bed *(rub eyes)*
To hear the things *(cup hand to ear)*
That Jesus said.

To the Temple
They would walk *(walk in place),*
So they could hear *(cup hand to ear)*
Lord Jesus talk.

Every day *(point to watch)*
This occurred.
And do you know *(shrug shoulders)*
What the people heard? *(Cup hand to ear.)*

They found the way
To be set free. *(Raise hands high.)*
Jesus said,
"Put your faith in me." *(Bow your head and fold hands in prayer.)*

After you've finished the story rhyme, give each child a sheet of paper. Have children roll their papers into cones, and use tape to hold the papers together.

Say: **In Bible times, people sometimes blew a sheep's horn to make a** trumpet sound. **The sheep's horn is called a shofar. We can blow the shofar to announce something special, or we can blow the shofar to warn people. Let's blow a single blast and hold it as long as possible. This meant that people should stop and listen.** Allow the children to make a trumpet sound. **Now let's blow three short toots on our horns. This also meant to stop and listen.** Allow the children to make this sound. **Now let's blow nine short toots. This was a sound of alarm or warning.** Allow the children to make this sound, helping them count to nine if necessary. Then allow the children to blow their horns as if they're announcing the Bible story.

The priest blew the shofar as a call for people to come to prayer and worship. (If you have a real shofar, you might want to bring it in and show it to the kids.)

Jesus knew God's house is a special place. Let's use blocks to make a courtyard kind of like the one Jesus taught and prayed in.

Framework

Give children the cardboard blocks. Allow the kids to place their blocks in a large U shape. Place the first block on the floor touching the wall on one side of your foam temple. Children can lay their blocks one against the other, like a train. The last block should fit up against the wall at the other side of the temple to complete the U shape. (Shift the blocks as necessary so that they'll fit.) Let children use pieces of masking tape to attach the blocks together on the top seams. (You may need to place tape on the bottom as well to hold the courtyard in place.) Ask:

• **Would you like to sit in our temple courtyard?**

Allow the children to take turns sitting inside the courtyard.

Say: **When Jesus was a boy, he listened to the teachers at the Temple and asked them questions. When Jesus was older, people came to the Temple to hear Jesus speak.**

Builders Banquet

Have kids wash their hands, then ask God to bless the snacks. Thank God for his house and a place to worship him.

Then let children use plastic knives to put frosting on graham crackers. Direct kids to place the cut licorice strings on the frosting to make temples with pillars. Tell children that God wants us to worship in his house, then let kids enjoy eating their snacks.

Bible-Town Tip

If you don't have cardboard blocks, stuff paper bags with newspaper. Then put another bag over the open end of each stuffed bag, and tape the bags together. You can also use shoe boxes or clean, empty cardboard milk cartons.

Dedication

Say: **Jesus liked being with God. So when he was in Jerusalem, where did he go? He went to the Temple. Now let's worship God in the temple courtyard that we made.**

Have kids find prayer partners and go over near your temple courtyard. Direct each pair to sit on the floor with their legs crossed, facing each other. Allow each partner to take the other partner's hands and move back and forth in a rowing motion. Encourage the children to sing the following song to the tune of "Row, Row, Row Your Boat."

Sing

Sing, sing, sing to God.
Sing and worship please.
I will worship you my God
For you're the one I need!

Then encourage children each to pray for their partner. Kids can pray, "God bless [child's name]. Please make [person's name] a worshipper like Jesus."

Additions

• Place chairs in a circle for all of the children. Play upbeat children's music, and have the kids pretend to play horns or trumpets while they walk around the chairs. Turn off the music, and have the children sit down. Call on a few children to shout out things they love about God. Turn on the music, and have kids play the game again. Be sure each child has a chance to share something about God.

• Give each preschooler a piece of blue or purple fabric. Have children hold the fabric over their faces and walk very carefully around the room. Explain that there was a curtain in the Temple that separated people from the holiest part. After Jesus died, the curtain ripped in two from top to bottom.

Have children each rip their piece of fabric in two. (You may need to start a tear with scissors beforehand.) Remind kids that Jesus' death made it so that we can be with God forever.

Rip another piece of fabric in half, stopping about one inch from the bottom. Use glue to attach the fabric to the smallest sheet of Styrofoam on the temple you made earlier.

Bible-Town Take-Home Page

I Worship…

Monday: Psalm 48:9, *I Worship a God of Love—*

Tuesday: Psalm 82:1-4, *I Worship a God Who Helps Me—*

Wednesday: Psalm 93:1-5, *I Worship a Strong and Mighty God—*

Thursday: Psalm 81:10, *I Worship a God Who Gives—*

Friday: Psalm 98:4-6, *I Worship a Real King—*

Saturday: Psalm 92:1-3, *I Worship a God Who Is With Me When I Sleep and When I Wake—*

Sunday: Psalm 24:7-10, *I Worship the King—*

In this lesson, kids learned that Jesus taught in the Temple (Luke 21:37-38) and that God wants us to worship in his house.

Hang up this calendar on the refrigerator or in another place where it will be easily seen. Read the Bible verse each day with your child, then have your child color the picture for that day.

Race for Jesus

Recreation in Bible Times

The Background

In the spring of A.D. 51, while he was in Corinth, Paul passed the Isthmian Games. The games were located about six miles from Corinth. It is possible that Paul used the site of these games to share an important lesson with the Corinthians.

Large crowds gathered for these games. The competitors came from places such as Corinth, Aegina, Thebes, and Athens. The Isthmian Games were held in honor of Poseidon (the god of the sea) and included athletic and musical competitions. There were separate competitions for men, youth, and boys. The athletic events included foot races, races in armor, discus and javelin throwing, wrestling, a regatta, and chariot races.

In this lesson, children will learn about some of the competitions in biblical times, and they'll learn that we should do our best for Jesus.

The Tools

- Bible
- large sheets of yellow or gold poster board
- several pairs of scissors
- copy of chariot picture (p. 71)
- 2 plastic toy wheelbarrows
- enough gold-colored cellophane to decorate the toy wheelbarrows
- 2 chairs
- a roll of masking tape
- copy of pictures of Jesus (p. 73)
- hole punches
- yarn

- crepe paper
- leaf patterns (p. 72) copied onto 8½x11 sheets of green paper
- a large package of chenille wires, any color
- vegetables cut into small pieces
- napkins
- a small cup of sports drink for each child

The Excavation

Before class, use the gold poster board, and cut out four ten- to twelve-inch round wheels. (Depending on the size of the toy wheelbarrows, you may need to vary the diameter of the wheels.) Also set out scissors, gold cellophane, and tape that you'll use later.

Photocopy the pictures of Jesus (p. 73), and make two paper signs that kids will wear around their necks. Punch holes at the top of each sign, and thread yarn through the holes.

Copy the leaf patterns (p. 72) onto sheets of green paper so that each child will have a set of leaves. Then set out the chenille wires, hole punches, and scissors.

The Project

Ribbon-Cutting

Have the children sit in a circle on the floor. Ask:

- **Does anybody know what a chariot is? What do you think a chariot looks like?**

Show kids the copy of the chariot picture (from page 71).

Say: **A chariot is like a wagon or a cart. In Bible times, kings rode chariots into war. They shot arrows at the enemy from the chariot too!** Ask:

- **Would you like to ride in a chariot?**

- **What do you think it would be like?**

Say: **People in Bible times played games using chariots.** Ask:

- **What games do you like to play?**

- **How do you think a chariot game is played?**

Say: **People sometimes had chariot races. We can have our own chariot races, but we'll need to decorate our chariots first. Chariots were sometimes decorated with gold, so let's put gold over our chariots.**

Bible-Town Tip

Use fairly short pieces of yarn for the signs so that the signs don't hang too loosely around children's necks as kids run the race.

Bible-Town Tip

For extra fun, set up a TV and VCR, and let children watch the clip that shows the chariots racing from the movie *The Prince of Egypt*.

Allow the children to help decorate the two wheelbarrows. Tape sheets of the gold cellophane onto the wheelbarrows as a gold covering. Then tape the large wheels onto the sides of each wheelbarrow.

Have the children form two teams. Direct each team to stand in a single-file line behind a piece of masking tape placed on the floor. Put a wheelbarrow at the start of each line. Then place two chairs on the other side of the room.

When you give the signal to begin, the child at the front of each line will push the "chariot" as fast as he or she can around the chair and back to the starting line. That child will give the chariot to the next team member as the game continues. Keep playing until all of the children have had a turn. Cheer and shout encouragement as children play.

Whistle While You Work

Say: **Athletes always try to do their best when they run or play games. And the Bible tells us that we should always do our best for Jesus. Now let's learn a song and jump and hop for Jesus.**

Lead the children through stretching exercises that begin with the legs and work up to the arms. Hold the stretches for ten seconds. Then sing the following song slowly to the tune of "Frère Jacques" as you do the motions in parentheses. Increase the tempo with each verse.

Be aware of any health problems, such as asthma, that the students may have. And be sure to allow enough room for the children to exercise without bumping into one another.

Sing

Warm up with me,
Warm up with me,
Stretch up tall. *(Reach up high.)*
Touch your toes. *(Touch toes.)*
Let's warm up together,
Let's warm up together,
Here we go. Here we go.

Work for Jesus!
Work for Jesus!
Hop like this *(hop up and down in place),*
Hop like that. *(Hop up and down in place.)*
Hop along for Jesus,
Hop along for Jesus,
Come, let's go! Come, let's go!

Work for Jesus!
Work for Jesus!
Jump, jump, jump. *(Jump up and down.)*
Jump, jump, jump. *(Jump up and down.)*
Jumping high for Jesus,
Jumping high for Jesus,
Come, let's go! Come, let's go!

Then have a cool-down time, and return to a slower tempo for the song. Allow the children to walk slowly around the exercise area as they sing the following verse.

Let's cool down now.
Let's cool down now.
Walk around.
Walk around.
We work hard for Jesus.
We work hard for Jesus.
Yes, we do! Yes, we do!

Blueprint

Have kids sit in a circle. Ask:

- **Did you work hard during our song?**

- **How does it feel to work hard?**

Open your Bible to 1 Corinthians 9:24 and say: **The Bible tells us in 1 Corinthians 9:24 that we should do our best for Jesus.** Ask:

- **What things can you do your best at?**

Say: **The Bible tells us about a man named Paul.** Have the children hold their palms together like a book. **He traveled to many places!** Tell kids to walk in place. **Paul told many people about Jesus.** Encourage kids to say to their friends, "Do you know about Jesus? Jesus loves you."

One day, Paul traveled near a place called Corinth. Suddenly he heard a lot of noise. Have kids place their hands at their ears and listen. **He saw many people!** Tell kids to place their hands above their eyes and look around. **Some people were running foot races.** Have the children run in place. **Some were having chariot races.** Tell kids to pretend to drive chariots and hold the reins. **Paul also saw people having horse races.** Have kids gallop in a circle like horses. **Paul even saw people training to be stronger.** Encourage kids to make muscles.

Paul wanted to tell the people something special! So he told them that in a race, all the runners run, but only one can win. We must run in such a way as to get the prize and win. When we try only for ourselves, we get a prize that won't last very long. But when we try our best for Jesus, we'll get a prize that lasts forever. Ask:

• **What kind of a prize do people usually get if they win a race?**

• **Can you think of some of the special things Jesus can give us?**

Say: **In Bible times, the winners of games and races received prizes. They got a crown to wear on their heads. It was a special crown of leaves. Let's make a leaf crown, then we can win prizes as we run our races later.**

Direct the children to the table where you've set out the supplies for making the crowns. Instruct the children to cut out the leaves. Next help them punch a hole at both ends of each leaf. Show the children how to twist the ends of about three chenille wires together to make one long wire. Next help the children each thread the wires through the holes in the leaves. Fit the leaf crown on the child's head before tying the ends of the wires together. Then spread out the paper leaves along the wires.

Say: **Now let's make a racetrack and run a race for Jesus.**

Framework

Allow children to help lay strips of the masking tape on the floor to make a track. Use the tape along two sides, like a road. (The size of the track and distance between the tape lines will depend on the amount of space you have in the room.)

Say: **Let's pretend that Paul is walking past our track. Pretend he's watching us race for Jesus. Let's show him how hard we can try for Jesus.** Ask:

• **When you do something well, who do you like to see it?**

• **How do you feel when other people like what you've done?**

Say: **Jesus wants to see you do your best. Let's run our best for Jesus.**

Have the children form two teams, and tell all of the children to remove their shoes. Allow the kids to take turns running on the track. Place one of the Jesus signs you made earlier around the neck of each runner. For fun, have two children hold up a piece of crepe paper across the end of the track. Allow the racers to run under the paper finish line.

Say: **Each runner will wear a sign around his or her neck. It will remind**

Bible-Town Tip

You may find that your children have difficulty cutting out the leaves. Consider purchasing leaves from a craft store or cutting the leaves out yourself before this lesson.

Your younger preschoolers may do better gluing the leaves to the chenille wires instead of punching holes in the leaves and threading the wires through. Cover a table with a plastic tablecloth if you decide to have kids glue the leaves to their crowns.

you to do your best as you run for Jesus. In Bible times, the people who won races got prizes. The prize was a crown of leaves. But when we go to heaven, Jesus will give us a crown that lasts forever.

Allow the children to wear their leaf crowns as prizes at the end of the race and during the snack time.

Builders Banquet

Before you begin, have the children wash their hands, then pray and ask God to bless the food. Ask him to make the children strong for him.

Say: **We will have a power-packed snack. God wants us to take good care of our bodies. Then we can do our best. We can eat veggies to make us strong. But Jesus is the real power, and we get our strength from him. Jesus is the one who helps us do our best.**

Hand out napkins, then serve vegetables cut into small pieces and sports drinks. Let kids eat and enjoy their snacks.

Dedication

Direct the children to a prayer walk on the racetrack as they sing the following song to the tune of "Old MacDonald Had a Farm." Allow two children to hold up crepe paper at the end of the track as the children walk underneath. Repeat the prayer until all the children have had a turn to walk down the track.

Sing

I will work hard each new day,
God, please hear me pray.
I'll do my best on each new day,
God, please hear me pray.
I'll love God's Word
And pray each day,
God, it's you that I'll obey.
I will work hard each new day.
God, please hear me pray.

At the end of the song, gather children in a group at the finish line.

Say: **Let's pray that we'll always love Jesus and that we'll never quit trying to do our best for him.**

Lead children in a prayer, and end with "In Jesus' name, amen."

Additions

• Have the children form two lines. Let kids stand on two tape marks on the floor, and have the children take turns tossing beanbags into two buckets. Explain that in Bible times, people played many games, and Jesus wanted them to do their best in everything. Let children pretend that their best is the beanbag. Then as they toss the beanbags into the buckets, they are giving their best to Jesus.

• Bring in two suits of child-sized, plastic armor. Have kids form two groups. Explain that in Bible times, people sometimes ran races while wearing armor. Armor protected them from arrows and other enemy weapons. Armor was heavy and made it hard for people to run. Help the two children who will be the first to race put on the armor. Let other children wear the armor and take turns running the course.

• Allow the children to take turns being human "chariots." Let one child lie on his or her stomach. Gently take the child's feet, and let the child walk forward on his or her hands.

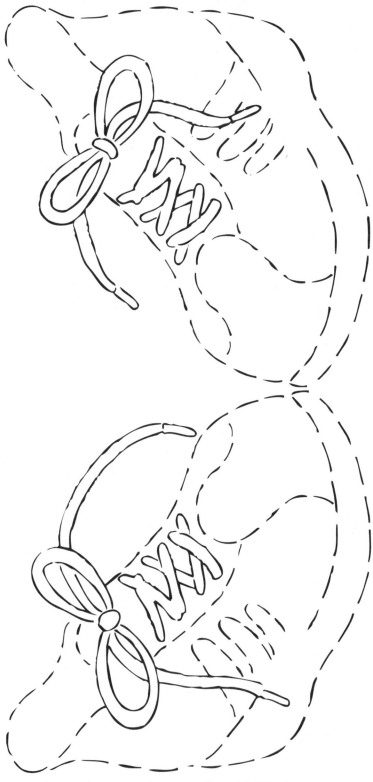

Today the kids heard about Paul's travels in Corinth and his advice to the Corinthians (1 Corinthians 9:24-27), and they learned that we should do our best for Jesus. Children also learned about some of the races that took place in biblical times.

Have your child trace the shoes with a glitter pen and then glue colorful shoelaces onto the paper. Pray and ask God to help you and your child do your best for Jesus.

Chariot

Leaf Patterns

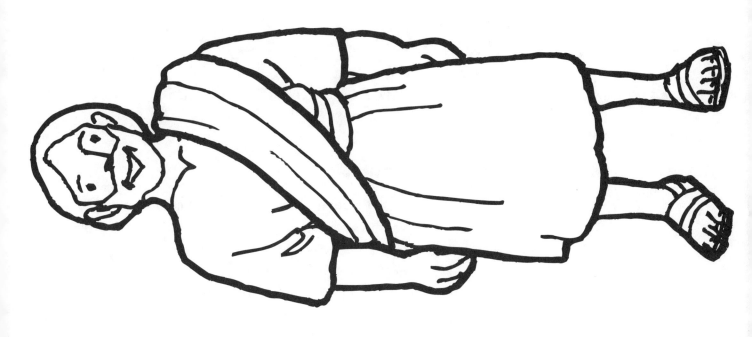

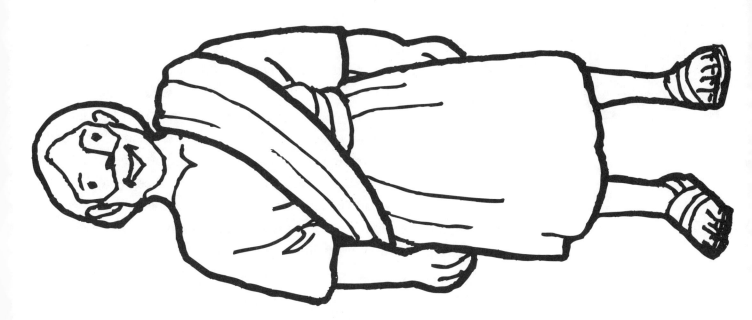

Neighing and Praying

Animals in Bible Times

The Foundation

God wants us to follow him.

Luke 15:1-7

The Background

From the first word of Creation, animals played a major role in man's existence. A rich man's wealth was measured in camels. God's prophet received food from ravens. A foolish man was rebuked by a donkey. A disheartened nation worshipped an idol in the form of a golden calf. And a lamb was offered in payment for disobedience. Through the centuries, animals have provided humans with transportation, food, clothing, labor, companionship, and have even borne sins in sacrifice. In return, God esteems the man who cares for the needs of his animals (Proverbs 12:10a). The shepherd was such a man.

A shepherd played an important role in biblical times. Early in the morning, the sheep would be led from the fold by the sound of the shepherd's voice. While some other animals must be driven, sheep will follow their master's voice. Always watchful for danger, the shepherd would bring his flock to pasture near a quiet stream or where water could be provided from troughs fed by wells. In the evening, the shepherd and his sheep would return to the fold, an enclosure built strong with stone. As the sheep entered the gate, each was recognized and counted. If a sheep was missing, the shepherd would secure the others in the fold and leave in search of the lost one. A good shepherd would give himself freely to find and rescue one of his flock.

A sheep's inability to fend for itself and its meek nature make it dependent upon the shepherd. The daily needs of sheep and the care given by the shepherd are tender pictures of our Lord. The Good Shepherd knows his flock by name, and those who hear his voice are wise to follow him. Like sheep to the shepherd, God's children are important and valued. Anyone who goes astray is earnestly sought and restored to the fold. God wants us to follow him.

The Tools

- Bible
- transparency of "Animal Silhouettes" (p. 83)
- overhead projector
- copy of "Simon the Sheep" picture (p. 84)
- scissors
- shepherd costume
- cardboard boxes of various sizes
- paper lunch sacks
- raisins
- string cheese
- portions of bread broken from a loaf
- fig cookies
- juice boxes
- copies of the "Sheep Finger Puppets" (p. 85)
- tape
- glue sticks
- cotton balls

The Excavation

Make a copy of "Animal Silhouettes" (p. 83) onto an overhead transparency, and set up an overhead projector. Then copy the "Simon the Sheep" picture (p. 84), and cut the two halves apart. Hide the picture that shows Simon the Sheep looking happy. Put it in a hiding place where the children are not likely to find it without some searching.

Ask an adult volunteer to portray the shepherd Zebulun. The volunteer should become familiar with the lines that he or she will speak to the children. Give the volunteer the picture that shows Simon the Sheep looking bewildered, and let Zebulun wear a shepherd costume.

Set out all the food items and lunch sacks to form an assembly line for children to make their snacks. Then copy and cut out sheep finger puppets for each child using the patterns on page 85.

The Project

Ribbon-Cutting

Have children sit in a circle.

Say: **God created all the animals when he made the world.** Ask:

• What's your favorite animal?

• What things do people use animals for today?

Say: **In Bible times, animals helped with work by carrying heavy loads in packs on their backs or by pulling plows. Animals were also used for food, and their fur or hair was used to make clothing.** Ask:

• **From what animals do we use hair, fur, or skin for our clothing?**

Say: **The wool from sheep can be used to make cloth. The strong skin of cows can be used to make shoes. Many animals that were used in Bible times are still used in the same way today. Let's play a game about all kinds of animals.**

Give the children the following clues and let them guess the name of the animal. Shine the "Animal Silhouettes" transparency on the wall, and let kids take turns pointing to the silhouettes when they answer.

I'm fun to ride,
When you say, "Giddyup," I go.
I'm a good worker,
And I stop when you say, "Whoa."
Who am I? *(Horse.)*

I live in the sea,
And I swallowed a man.
The man's name was Jonah,
Can you guess what I am?
Who am I? *(Fish or whale.)*

On my back I have a hump,
And I travel the desert land.
I can go a long way without water
In a long caravan.
Who am I? *(Camel.)*

You hear me say, "Heehaw"
When you ride on my back.
I have very large ears,
And I can carry a pack.
Who am I? *(Donkey.)*

I'm plump, round, and furry.
I walk and prowl.
If you come near my cubs,
You'll hear me growl.
Who am I? *(Bear.)*

I follow the shepherd,
He keeps me safe at night,
My fur is called wool.
I'm fuzzy and white.
Who am I? *(Sheep.)*

Remind the children that animals were very important to the people in biblical times. Animals made life easier by helping with the hard work and by providing food and clothing.

Say: **One of the most important animals was the sheep. God said that people who treated their animals kindly were very wise. Shepherds loved their sheep and took good care of them.** Ask:

   • **Do you have pets at home?**

   • **How do you care for them?**

   • **If you lived in Bible times, what kind of animal would you like to have for your own?**

   • **How would you care for it?**

Whistle While You Work

Teach children the following song to the tune of "Mary Had a Little Lamb," and add children's names during the second verse.

Sing

The shepherd has a field of sheep,
Field of sheep, field of sheep.
The shepherd has a field of sheep
In Wee-Built Bible Town.

Jesus has a little lamb,
Little lamb, little lamb.
Jesus has a little lamb,
And [child's name] is his [or her] name.

Blueprint

Open your Bible to Luke 15:1-7, and say: **In Luke 15, Jesus told a story to help people understand God's love. He told a story about a shepherd who had a hundred sheep. The shepherd knew each one of his sheep by sight. He knew the woolly ones and the skinny ones. He knew the spotted ones and the white ones. And each sheep had a name.**

Let each child choose a sheep name and pretend to be a sheep. Pause periodically as you teach the following information, and let the kids act out what you've described.

Say: **As the shepherd walked, his sheep would follow him. The flock was counted every morning and again at night. One, two, three, four, five—all the way to a hundred. If a sheep was missing, the shepherd would go out to look for the one lost sheep. It didn't matter that he had ninety-nine other sheep left. He cared for the lost one as much as the ones that were safe. The shepherd would walk many miles and climb up and down dangerous trails calling for his sheep. The shepherd would listen and watch. When he found the sheep at last, he would carry it safely home. His friends and neighbors would rejoice with him for finding the sheep.**

At this point, the volunteer playing Zebulun should enter the classroom and quietly begin looking behind chairs and in corners, making it obvious that he or she is searching for something. After catching the children's attention, Zebulun can say the following lines.

Zebulun: **Excuse me, kids. I'm Zebulun, a shepherd, and I'm looking for one of my sheep. Have you seen anything white and fluffy pass through here? His name is Simon. He's very cute. He has floppy ears and a little tail. He looks like, well, you know, like a sheep. Just a minute, I think I have a picture of him...Here it is.** Have Zebulun hold up the picture that shows a bewildered Simon the Sheep. **This is my sheep Simon. I've looked under bushes and behind rocks and up and down the hills. He's here in Wee-Built Bible Town somewhere. Have you seen him?** Allow the children time to respond.

I have a hundred sheep. They're all important to me, but I've left the other ninety-nine in a safe place to go find this one that's lost. If you see Simon, will you let me know? Better yet, will you help me look for him before

he does some silly sheep thing and gets himself hurt? You can all be my shepherd's helpers. Help me look around the room and let's see if we can find the picture of Simon the Sheep.

When the children find the picture of the happy Simon, ask them to come back and sit down together. Zebulun should thank the children for helping.

Say: **It's a very dangerous thing for a sheep to be off on its own. A sheep is helpless to defend itself against wild animals, and it can't find its way back to the other sheep. A sheep needs the shepherd to feed it and protect it from danger like steep cliffs.** Ask:

- **How do you think a shepherd feels when he realizes that one of his sheep is lost?**

- **What could happen to the sheep without the shepherd to take care of it?**

- **What would a shepherd do as soon as he knew a sheep was missing?**

Say: **Jesus is like a shepherd, and we are like the sheep. Some sheep stay with the shepherd, and that's a good thing. But some wander away and get lost. Jesus wants us to follow him every day. If we do, he will care for us. If we run away from Jesus' ways, he is sad, but he will come to where we are and show us the way back to him.** Ask:

- **Have you ever been lost in a store?**

- **How did you feel?**

- **How might a sheep feel when it is lost?**

- **How does Jesus take care of us—like a shepherd takes care of his sheep?**

Framework

Say: **We live in houses, and our houses give us a safe place to rest and play. If you were a sheep, you would sleep in a place called a *sheepfold*. A sheepfold is a fenced-in area with a gate. The fence is not made of wood or wire, but of rocks piled up—it's very strong and sturdy. Let's make a strong sheepfold that could protect sheep from wild animals.**

Using a corner of your room where two walls can be used as part of the construction, let the children stack the boxes to make the other two walls. Leave an opening for a gate.

Say: **Shepherds come in all shapes and sizes. There are old shepherds and young shepherds. Sometimes there are even a few girl shepherds. Some shepherds who are nomads take their flocks from one grazing area to another. Others live in villages.**

Designate a few of your children to be shepherds, and let the other kids pretend to be sheep. As you tell the children the following things about the shepherds in biblical times, let them act out each action you explain. Tell kids that shepherds lived with and protected their sheep. At night, the sheep were placed inside the safe walls of the sheepfold. The shepherd often slept by the door so that wild animals could not get by him and attack the sheep. A good shepherd was ready to fight for his sheep. During the day, the shepherd led the sheep out of the sheepfold so that the sheep could have grass to eat.

Say: **The sheep were important to the shepherd. Jesus said that he is our shepherd, and we are important to Jesus. He cares for us and wants us to follow him. If we wander away, Jesus comes to find us and will help us learn to stay close to him.**

Builders Banquet

Have kids wash their hands and sit in the snack area. Ask:

- **Have you ever packed a lunch?**

- **What do you like to eat for lunch?**

Say: **The shepherd carried several days' food supply in a bag. Their food consisted of bread, cheese, olives, raisins, and sometimes figs.**

Help your class make lunches like a shepherd might have made. Give children each a paper lunch sack, and direct them to where the food is set out. After the kids have put their snack items into their bags, have them sit together near your sheepfold. Then lead the children in a brief prayer.

Say: **Lord, thank you for giving us good food to eat and for taking care of us every day. In Jesus' name, amen.**

Remind your class that the shepherd would always make sure that his sheep had plenty of food. He would also bring them to a place where they could drink water. Sheep are easily frightened and will not drink from a stream if the water is rushing by too quickly. Give the kids their juice boxes, and ask them to listen for you to whisper as you play this game. When they hear you whisper "Quiet water, quiet water," they may drink. When you say, "Rushing water, rushing water" in a loud voice, they must not drink.

After playing the game and eating for a few minutes, say: **Jesus is like a shepherd. He cares for us by giving us good food, clothing, and safe places to live. When you sit down at your table tonight, you can thank your Good Shepherd, Jesus, for giving you lots of good things to eat and drink. When you get into bed tonight, you can thank Jesus for giving you a safe, warm place to sleep.** Ask:

- **What are some of the things Jesus, the Good Shepherd, has given you?**

Dedication

Give each child up to five sheep puppets (the patterns are on page 85). Direct children to glue a small piece of cotton to each of their sheep, then help children tape the puppets together so that the puppets fit on the children's fingers. Have the children slip the puppets onto the fingers of one hand. Follow the finger play together.

The Good Shepherd knows his sheep. *(Hold up fingers.)*
He calls them all by name. *(Wiggle fingers.)*
And if they run away from him *(lower hand with puppets),*
He calls them back again. *(Raise fingers.)*

Say: **Let's pray and thank the Lord.**

Dear Lord,

You are my shepherd, and I am one of your sheep. Thank you for loving me and caring for me. Help me to follow you by obeying you every day.

In Jesus' name, amen.

Additions

• Using a portable cassette recorder, let the children create a tape of sounds that Bible-times animals would make. Then play the tape, and let children take turns guessing the animal sounds.

• Show the "Animal Silhouettes" transparency on the wall. Point to one of the animals, and let the children pretend to be that animal. Continue playing, and let kids try to act out all of the animals.

• Turn on the overhead projector, and place the "Animal Silhouettes" transparency on it. Then turn off the projector light and cover up one of the animals. Turn the projector light back on, and let the children guess which animal is missing.

Bible-Town Take-Home Page

Today kids heard the parable of the lost sheep (Luke 15:1-7), and they learned to follow the Good Shepherd.

Give your child several cotton balls to glue onto the sheep picture. Once the glue is dry, play a game of Hide and Go Sheep. Hide the sheep picture, and let your child be the shepherd. A good shepherd seeks the sheep that is missing and brings it safely back.

The next time your child asks to play Follow the Leader, play Follow the Shepherd instead, and take turns being the sheep and the shepherd. Remind your child that Jesus, the Good Shepherd, wants us to follow him.

Animal Silhouettes

Simon the Sheep

Bewildered

Simon the Sheep

Happy

Sheep Finger Puppets

Tape Here

Tape Here

Giddyup Little Donkey

Transportation in Bible Times

The Foundation

God wants us to know that Jesus is our Savior.

Mark 11:1-10

The Background

In biblical times, people didn't often travel very far from home. If they did, it was for trade or for religious celebrations. How and where people could travel depended a lot on the availability of roads and water. People chose how they would travel based on how far they had to go, what they had to carry, and how far an animal could go without needing water. In the same way, we now have to figure out how far our cars can go between stops for gasoline.

In biblical times, most people walked. Walking was cheap and available to almost everyone. People also commonly traveled using donkeys, because donkeys could be ridden and used as pack animals. Donkeys could carry huge loads for their size, and they were sure-footed on rocky terrain. Donkeys are still used today for traveling in rural places.

Riding on a donkey was a mark of both prestige and power. Today, we would think a horse would be more regal, but in Bible times, the horse was associated with war.

In this lesson, children will hear the story about Jesus' triumphal entry, and they'll learn that Jesus is our Savior.

The Tools

- Bible
- gray socks
- black felt
- black yarn
- needle
- scissors
- glue

- black markers
- plates and napkins
- pineapple rings
- plastic knife
- shredded coconut
- red, yellow, and green food coloring
- resealable plastic bag
- shallow bowl
- stick pretzels
- chocolate chips

The Excavation

For each child in your class, cut two small triangles of black felt. (Kids will use the felt as ears for their sock puppets.) Also, you can use a needle to thread lengths of black yarn through the gray socks (as described on page 89) if you'd rather not take class time to do this later. Then set all of the materials for the sock puppets on a table where the kids will work.

The Project

Ribbon-Cutting

Play a game to help the children identify what it means to travel and how we travel today.

Say: **Pretend you're going to visit your grandparents or some of your other relatives. When I point to you, show me how you will travel to their house.** Start the game yourself, then let the children each take a turn. Kids could pretend to drive a car, take a bus, fly in an airplane, take a train, or walk.

We're going to learn how people traveled back in Bible times and how Jesus traveled when he went into Jerusalem. The way Jesus chose to travel tells us a lot about him! But first, let's sing a song about Jesus.

Whistle While You Work

Sing this song to the tune of "London Bridge," and have kids stand up and clap to the beat as they sing. Fill in each verse with a different attribute. Stop clapping for the last word, and have kids act out the attribute.

Sing

Jesus is so many things,
So many things, so many things.
Jesus is so many things!
He is...

...**powerful.** *(Flex muscles.)*
...**gentle.** *(Pretend to be rocking a baby.)*
...**God.** *(Raise arms to the sky.)*
...**man.** *(Put your arms out to the side.)*
...**perfect.** *(Put your hands on your waist.)*
...**forgiving.** *(Pat your neighbor on the back.)*

Blueprint

Say: **In Bible times, people didn't have cars or trains. They didn't even have bicycles. Do you know how they got around? Most of the time they walked. And sometimes they rode horses or donkeys.**

Today's Bible story talks about a very special time when Jesus rode on a donkey. He was riding into a city called Jerusalem. A crowd of people welcomed him by cheering and waving branches because they thought he was their new king. Read Mark 11:1-10 from an easy-to-understand translation.

Then let kids act out Jesus' triumphal entry into Jerusalem. Have children form two lines facing each other with a pathway between them. Encourage children to take turns pretending to be Jesus riding a donkey by "galloping" along or even riding on your back. Tell the kids in the "crowd" to spread their fingers apart and wave their arms like palm branches. Have children say, "Hosanna! Blessed is he who comes in the name of the Lord!"

Say: **In Bible times, riding on a donkey was a sign of being powerful, but it was also a sign of peace. So when Jesus rode into Jerusalem on a donkey, he showed everyone that he was a powerful king and a gentle king. By riding on a donkey, Jesus helped the people to know that he is our Savior.**

Framework

Say: **Let's each make a sock puppet donkey to remind us of the time Jesus rode into Jerusalem on a donkey.**

Give each child a clean gray sock. Demonstrate how they can put their hands inside the socks to make simple puppets. Show kids where you've set out the black yarn, glue, the felt triangles, and markers. Then show children where to draw eyes on each puppet with a marker, glue on a mane made of the yarn, and glue on two felt triangles as ears. Help children put the items in about the right locations, but don't push kids for perfection. Write the child's initials inside his or her sock.

Use a needle to thread a piece of yarn into the side of each puppet's mouth and out through the other side. (Make sure the needle is never within the reach of children.) "Tie up" the donkeys by wrapping the yarn around doorknobs, a banister, or other objects that can be used as hitching posts.

Lead the group to the other side of the room and have them huddle together. Say: **Jesus needs a donkey! Who will go over and get one for me?** Send a volunteer over to get his or her donkey and run back. Let the child put the puppet on his or her hand, and have the puppet walk through the crowd of preschoolers. Encourage the crowd to let the donkey through while they shout and cheer for Jesus. Give all of the children an opportunity to run and untie their donkeys.

Builders Banquet

Let the children make furry donkeys for snacks! As children are washing their hands, make brown coconut by placing one cup of shredded coconut in a plastic bag. Mix about ½ teaspoon of water with 3 drops of red, 1 drop of green, and 2 drops of yellow food coloring. Add this mixture to the coconut. Shake until the coconut turns brown, and put the coconut in a shallow bowl.

Cut the pineapple rings in half. Give each child a plate and a napkin, then give each child a pineapple-ring half and allow the children to roll the pineapple in the brown coconut. Then have children each stick a pretzel stick through the pineapple to make the donkey's neck.

Make heads for the donkeys by cutting the extra pineapple-ring halves in half again. Use one of these pieces for each donkey's head. Have children roll the pineapple pieces in brown coconut, and put the pineapple on top of the pretzel neck. Let children each add a chocolate chip for an eye. Have kids say the following prayer, and let them eat and enjoy their treats!

Dedication

Before kids eat their snacks, take a minute to pray and thank God for sending Jesus.

Dear God,

Thank you for sending Jesus! Thank you that Jesus is...

...God *and* man,

...powerful *and* gentle,

...perfect *and* forgiving.

In Jesus' name, amen.

Additions

• Make a hitching post for the donkey puppets by taping two cardboard wrapping paper tubes to the wall. Mount a third tube at the top of the other tubes to form a crossbar, and tie up the donkeys in your little Bible town.

• You may wish to have a traveling banquet. Put snacks, such as crackers, apples, raisins, and dates, in various locations around the room. Then let kids pretend to be in a traveling caravan and stop to eat the treats.

Bible-Town Take-Home Page

Today kids learned about Jesus and his triumphal entry into Jerusalem (Mark 11:1-10), and they learned that God wants us to know that Jesus is our Savior. Children also found out about transportation in biblical times.

Fold a piece of paper in half and then in half again. Staple along the fold on the long side. Cut along the folds on the top edge to make a book.

On the cover write, "Jesus is…"

On each set of facing pages write two attributes, and have your child draw pictures to illustrate them. For example, you might use "God and man," "powerful and gentle," and "perfect and forgiving." Help your child think of ways to illustrate each attribute. For example, he or she could draw a child showing off his or her muscles for "powerful" and a person petting a lamb for "gentle."

Consider making similar books for each person in your family. You might want to put the family member's picture on the front of his or her book.

Strings, Flutes, and Tambourines

Music in Bible Times

The Foundation

God is delighted when we praise him.

Psalm 150

The Background

In the Old Testament, music was an integral part of Hebrew life, particularly in the areas of worship, military life, and daily social interactions. This lesson is directed at the worship or praise aspect of music. Among the many instruments used in worship, most can be placed in three categories: stringed instruments which were strummed or plucked; wind instruments which were blown into; and percussion instruments which were struck or shaken.

Percussion instruments brought a base of rhythm to the music. Stringed instruments may have originated from hearing the sound of a bowstring as it was released, and perhaps wind instruments were devised after hearing wind blow through a hollow structure such as a reed. Each category of instrument contributes a unique type of sound that brings rhythm, melody, and harmony to the finished product of praise music. All three types of instruments—stringed, percussion, and wind—are included in the great psalm of praise, Psalm 150.

The music was spirited, and singing and dancing were often added as participants celebrated God's love and providence. This lesson will help children learn that God is delighted when we praise him.

The Tools

- Bible
- instruments such as a guitar, horn, and cymbals
- cloth
- heavy paper plates, 2 for each child

- stapler
- various types of dry cereal
- colorful stickers and markers
- hole punch
- ribbons
- freestanding coat rack with several hooks
- cookies, 2 for each child
- gumdrops, 2 for each child
- frosting
- resealable plastic bags
- scissors

The Excavation

Set the instruments on the table and cover them with the cloth. Then set up the coat rack; it will function as the "temple tambourine tree" for storing the tambourines the children will make.

Fill a few small, resealable plastic bags with frosting, and seal the bags tightly.

The Project

Ribbon-Cutting

Say: **Hi, kids! Welcome to our time of praise. I'm so glad you're here today! We're going to have a lot of fun learning about the music of people who lived in Bible times. We're also going to make our own instruments. But first, let's play a game to show how we can make music with our hands. Watch what I do, and then do the same actions. Let's see if you can keep up.**

Have kids form a circle on the floor. Clap your hands together twice, and have kids copy your actions. Clap your hands together once and slap your knees twice, and have kids copy you again. Move the game along by creating variations, such as making a beat on a tabletop, patting your head, or patting your tummy—any silly combination to get kids smiling! Play the game at different speeds and create an atmosphere of fun.

Say: **Wow! You did a terrific job.** Ask:

• **Do you think that you were making music? Why or why not?**

Say: **You can make music in many different ways. Clapping is just one way to make music.** Ask:

• **Besides clapping, how else do you think we can make music to praise God?**

Say: **Let me teach you a fun song, and then you can help me sing it.**

Whistle While You Work

Teach children the following song. Later in the lesson they'll be able to sing the song as they play the instruments they've made.

Say: **Listen carefully to the words of this song and see if you can think of some other ways to praise God with music.** Sing the following song to the tune of "Jesus Loves Me."

Sing

Play the trumpet and the flute.
I can praise God—so can you.
Praise God using harps and strings.
Praise with cymbals 'n' tambourines.

Let's play and praise God.
Let's play and praise God.
Let's play and praise God.
We praise in many ways.

Sing the song several times until the kids become familiar with it. Let the children have some fun as they imitate the instrument sounds.

Say: **That was fantastic! You are all wonderful singers! First we made music by clapping, then we praised God with singing. Our song also told some other ways to praise God with music. Do you remember them?** Allow children to respond. **We can praise God with instruments such as horns, harps, and tambourines. Let's look at how different instruments are played to praise God.**

Blueprint

Have the instruments on a table next to you, but covered with the cloth.

Say: **God loves it when we praise him. He wants to hear us and see us show our love for him. The Bible tells us about many ways that people praised God. Listen as I read Psalm 150 to see if you can hear the names of any instruments.** Read Psalm 150:3-5 from an easy-to-read translation. Ask:

• **Can you pick out the names of the musical instruments? What instrument is this one like?** Hold up a guitar.

• **Which instrument is this?** Hold up a horn.

• **What are these?** Hold up cymbals.

Say: **This next part is a little harder. Each one of these is a certain kind of** instrument. **People in Bible times praised God with stringed instruments** (pick up the guitar) **kind of like a guitar, wind instruments** (pick up the horn) **like this horn, and percussion instruments** (pick up the cymbals) **like these cymbals. All of these instruments make different kinds of sound when you play them.**

Have children come up and gently explore and play the instruments. You might want to hold each instrument while children investigate. Then play a worship song on one of the instruments, or invite a musician to come in and play a worship song.

Say: **In Bible times, people worshipped God with instruments that were a lot like some of the instruments we use today to worship God.** Ask:

• **Why do we use instruments when we worship God?**

Say: **In Bible times, people used instruments to worship God because the instruments gave a different, fun sound, and they helped bring everyone together. We use instruments today because we want to give God our best, and we want everyone to be able to join in worshipping God.**

Framework

Each child will make a tambourine. Set out heavy paper plates of different colors. Allow the children each to pick two plates, and have kids write their names on their plates. Demonstrate how to set one plate on the table and sprinkle dry cereal on it until the cereal covers the face of the plate.

Lay the second plate over the first plate, and staple the plates together. Then let the children use stickers and markers to decorate their plates if they wish. Punch a hole in the edge of each tambourine. Let each child choose a piece of ribbon. Slip the ribbon through the hole and tie it. Then use the ribbon to hang the tambourine from a hook on the coat rack. The coat rack will serve as a "temple tambourine tree" where the children can keep their tambourines. While kids are working, you might want to sing the praise song that was learned earlier.

Let the kids experiment with the tambourines for a few minutes.

Builders Banquet

Have kids wash their hands before they make their treats.

Say: **Let's put the instruments down for a little while. We'll have a chance to use them again in a few minutes. But now it's time for our snacks! In fact, you can help make the snacks—they're kind of like "snack instruments."** Give each child two cookies and two gumdrops.

We're going to make "cookie cymbals." We'll put a bit of frosting on the back of each cookie, and then stick the gumdrop in the frosting. This will

Bible-Town Tip

Feel free to substitute instruments as needed for this activity. For example, if you don't have cymbals, use drumsticks or even a pan and a wooden spoon.

make a "handle" for the cymbals. Snip off a corner of each bag of frosting, and help kids squeeze a bit of frosting onto each cookie.

Thank God for the food, then let children eat their snacks.

Dedication

Have children get their tambourines. Say: **Let's praise God with music. Let's sing the song we learned earlier. Sing the first verse with me, and then we'll play our instruments. Are you ready?**

Repeat the song kids learned in the "Whistle While You Work" activity. Encourage kids to play their tambourines and make a joyful noise to the Lord.

Say: **See how much fun it can be to praise God? I know he loves watching and listening to you make music for him. Let's take a minute and pray about that right now. Do what I do as we pray.**

> **Thank you, God, that you made music.** *(Pretend to strum a guitar or play a horn.)*
>
> **We're thankful that we can praise you with beautiful sounds.** *(Cup hands to your ears.)*
>
> **Thank you for loving us and taking care of us.** *(Shake tambourines and shout "Hooray!")*
>
> **And for sending Jesus to save us.** *(Bow head.)*
>
> **In Jesus' name we pray, amen.**

Additions

• You'll need some lightweight plastic pipes with an interior diameter of one-half inch. Have kids work together to measure and mark the following lengths of pipe (in inches): 3¼, 3⅜, 3¾, 4⅛, 4¾, 5¼, 6, 6½. Help the kids place the measured pipes in a vise. Have an adult helper cut the pipes on the measured lines with a fine-toothed hacksaw. Then let kids rub the cut ends of the pipes with rough sandpaper until all of the ends are smooth.

Demonstrate how to play a pipe. Press the pipe against your bottom lip. Press one thumb against the bottom of the pipe to cover it completely. Blow across the tube. The shorter, higher-pitched pipes tend to be a bit easier to play than the longer ones. Let each child choose a pipe to play. Arrange the children and their pipes from the lowest to the highest sound.

Cutting the pipes according to the given measurements will result in a set of eight pipes that comes reasonably close to producing a major scale. You may want to "tune" a pipe to a higher pitch by cutting or sanding it off a bit.

Bible-Town Take-Home Page

Today kids learned about praising the Lord with music (Psalm 150), and they learned that God is delighted when we praise him.

Create a family band! Your preschooler can involve the entire family in making praise music. Use instruments that you already have, or clap, whistle, and create your own unique instruments.

You might use buckets or pans as drums and wooden spoons as drumsticks. You could also fill several water glasses with different amounts of water and tap the glasses with a spoon. You could even stretch a rubber band between two objects and strum it.

You can also make your own instrument using buttons and cardboard. Cut a 1x4-inch piece of cardboard, and glue a button near each end. Then fold the cardboard piece in the middle. When the cardboard is clicked together, the buttons will hit each other to make "music."

Once each family member has an instrument, make a joyful noise to the Lord!

Celebrate!

Holidays in Bible Times

The Foundation

God wants us to make him the center of our celebrations.

Leviticus 23:33-44

The Background

In Bible times, holidays were called feasts. These were times to rejoice and celebrate. There were some common themes to these feasts: acknowledgement of sin, devotion to God, and sacrifices to signify the forgiveness of sin and reconciliation with God. There are many different feasts mentioned in the Bible. Some of these are the Feast of Unleavened Bread (Leviticus 23:6-8), the Feast of Weeks (Leviticus 23:15-22), and the Feast of Tabernacles (Leviticus 23:33-43).

For the Feast of Unleavened Bread, God said that for seven days the people were to eat bread made without yeast. Each day they were to give offerings to God, and on the first and last days, they would gather together to worship. This feast commemorated the Israelites' deliverance from Egypt. God's people had been slaves in Egypt, and when they finally were able to leave, they had to go quickly, and there was no time for the bread to rise.

The Feast of Weeks (also called the Feast of Harvest or the Day of First Fruits), was a day on which the Israelites gave offerings to God, including the first fruits of the wheat harvest. The whole community came together, and it was a day of rest from the normal work. At the end of the description of this feast in the Bible, there is a command from God to leave part of the harvest for the poor (Leviticus 23:22).

The Feast of Tabernacles (also called the Feast of Booths) celebrated the harvest. This feast lasted seven days, and the first and last days were days of community worship and celebration. The harvest and produce were gathered, and people lived in booths, or temporary shelters made of branches. This feast was a reminder that the Israelites had lived in tents after leaving Egypt and a reminder of the rich harvest in the Promised Land.

Isaiah 1:11-20 shows that God was not pleased with the way the feasts had become. This was not because God didn't ordain feasts, but because many Israelites had moved away from the feasts' spiritual purposes. The Israelites did what God commanded *outwardly*, but their hearts were not right.

God doesn't want us to just go through the motions. Instead, he wants our hearts and minds to be focused on him and on what is right, pure, and holy.

This is interesting! Our modern-day holidays of Jesus' birth and resurrection have become focused on many things—Santa, presents, Easter eggs, bunnies— sometimes the *least* of which is God.

It's an important message for little ones to hear and remember: Make God the center of your celebrations!

The Tools

- Bible
- refrigerator box (or several large boxes)
- utility knife
- several tan or green bedsheets
- pictures of holiday images
- crackers
- small squares of bread
- wheat stalk (from a craft store or florist) or bag of flour
- plastic knives
- large chunks of fruit
- paper plates
- napkins

The Excavation

Use a utility knife to cut off the flaps from the top and bottom of a refrigerator box so that kids will be able to crawl inside the box. Then cut up different kinds of fruit into chunks, and remove the seeds.

The Project

Ribbon-Cutting

Drape a sheet over several chairs to make a tent for this attention-getting activity. Have children sit with you in the tent. Ask:

- **Has anyone ever been in a tent?**

- **What are tents used for?**

Say: **In Bible times, some people lived in tents, and tents were also used for a celebration called the Feast of Tabernacles.** *Tabernacle* **is a fancy name for a tent.** Have the children practice saying "tabernacle."

Hold up several holiday pictures, such as a Christmas tree, a Thanksgiving turkey, an Easter egg, and a heart. Ask the children to name the holidays associated with the images and explain why we celebrate them.

Say: **Today, we're going to learn about a Bible-times holiday that Jesus would have celebrated. It's called the Feast of Tabernacles. During the holiday, people had a big feast and lived in a tent, or tabernacle. Today, we're going to make our own Bible-times tent. We're also going to learn what God thinks is most important about holidays. But first, let's start by learning a song.**

Whistle While You Work

Sing this song to the tune of "Old MacDonald Had a Farm," and have kids do the motions given in the parentheses. This will help the children to remember the words—and the message!

Sing

God our Father gave us feasts! Yes, he really did! (*Raise your arms and point to heaven.*)

God our Father gave us feasts! Yes, he really did! (*Raise your arms and point to heaven.*)

With Christmas here, and Easter there (*cradle a baby, then make a cross with your arms*),

Here a prayer, there a praise (*fold your hands in prayer, then raise your hands*),

Thank you God for holidays! (*Put arms straight out with hands open.*)

God our Father gave us feasts! Yes, he really did! (*Raise your arms and point to heaven.*)

Sing this song several times. After you have practiced, you may want to assign each child one line. Be sure you sing with each child when it's his or her turn. Then have kids stand in a circle and sing the song again.

Blueprint

Have the children wash their hands before this activity.

Say: **Today we get to learn about a few Bible-times holidays and celebrate one of them in a tent that we're going to make! God told his people about lots of holidays to celebrate. These celebrations helped remind the people of the amazing things God had done for them.**

Pass out a cracker and a small square of bread to each child. Ask:

- **What are some differences between the cracker and the piece of bread?**

- **Which would you rather eat? Why?**

Invite the children to eat the samples and explain the difference in taste.

Say: **One holiday that God told his people to celebrate was called the Feast of Unleavened Bread. Unleavened bread is a little bit like crackers. This holiday was to remind the Israelites that God had led them out of slavery in Egypt. The Israelites had been forced to stay and work in Egypt for a mean king, and God's people were finally allowed to go. But they had to go quickly, and they didn't have time to let their bread dough rise and get fluffy. So they just had to have flat bread.**

Hold up a stalk of wheat or a small bag of flour. Ask the children to guess what it is. Say: **Another holiday that God asked his people to celebrate was called the Feast of Weeks. During this holiday, the people gave thanks to God for the wheat harvest. This feast is similar to the one that we're going to celebrate today—the Feast of Tabernacles. Let's read about the Feast of Tabernacles in our Bible.**

Open your Bible to Leviticus 23:33-44, and summarize the passage.

Say: **The Feast of Tabernacles lasted for seven days. The first day was a day for a gathering and celebration. To celebrate, God asked the people to take fruit and palm branches and rejoice! This celebration probably included singing and waving the palm branches. Then for seven days the Israelites were to camp out in tents and give offerings to God. The last day was a day of rest and a time for the Israelites to gather and give offerings. This holiday reminded people of the time God led the Israelites safely out of Egypt and the Israelites lived in tents.**

There is one thing that all of these celebrations have in common—praising God! Whenever we celebrate a holiday, we should always put God at the center of our celebration!

Framework

Lay a refrigerator box on its side, and drape a sheet over the box. Lead children into the "tent" and say: **When God's people left Egypt, they had to live in tents. God gave the Israelites a home—just like he gives people places to live today. Let's thank God for our homes.**

As each child goes out of the tent, have him or her say a prayer of thanks for the homes God has given us.

Builders Banquet

Before children begin, have them wash their hands. Then give each child a paper plate with his or her name on it, a napkin, several large chunks of fruit, and a plastic knife. The fruit can include apples, pears, and oranges. Make sure you've removed the seeds, and give the children fruit that has already been cut into large chunks. Ask the children to prepare the fruit by cutting it into smaller bite-sized pieces. If you wish, you can add a couple of dips to the plates to make a fancier feast. Yogurt or softened cream cheese would work well.

Have kids eat their snacks as part of the "Dedication" activity that follows.

Dedication

Dedicate your new Bible-times tent to God by re-enacting the Feast of Tabernacles. Pretend to do the steps that are listed in the Bible verses in Leviticus. You might do something like this:

- Have the children leave their fruit plates on a table.

- Tell kids to gather in a circle outside the tent.

- Hold hands and say this prayer:

Dear God,

Thank you for creating holidays for us to celebrate! Help us to always keep you at the center of our celebrations. We dedicate our Bible-times tent to you.

In Jesus' name, amen.

- Let kids sing songs and wave real palm branches or make-believe palm branches—their arms and fingers!

- Have children each eat one piece of fruit from their plate.

- Encourage kids to pretend to go to sleep in or near the tent.

- Repeat the previous two steps several times to represent the seven days. (Eat a piece of fruit, then pretend to sleep.)

- Have kids gather one last time to sing, wave palm branches, and praise God!

Additions

- For this lesson, you may want to set up a small camping tent to remind kids of the tents they use today. Have them imagine what living in a tent for a long time would be like.

- Palm branches were used during the Feast of Tabernacles. Ask a florist for some palm branches that kids can wave when they sing and praise God!

- You may wish to make your own palm branches instead. Have the children trace each other's hands on green construction paper, and cut these shapes out. Tape the "palm fronds" to craft sticks, and let kids use them at your Feast of Tabernacles celebration.

Bible-Town Take-Home Page

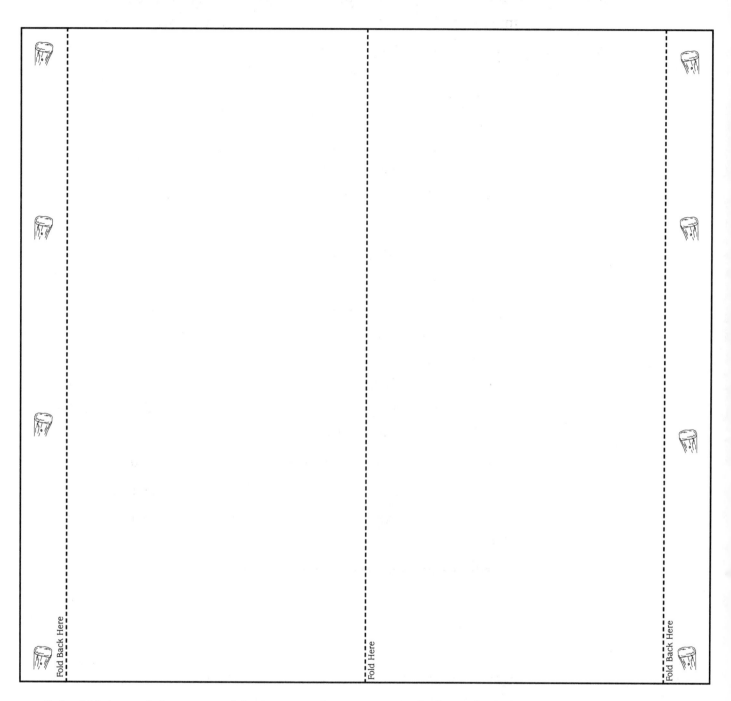

Fold Back Here

Fold Here

Fold Back Here

Today kids learned about some of the important feasts in the Bible, and they learned that God wants us to make him the center of our celebrations.

To remind your child of the lesson, make your own miniature Bible-times tent. Have your child decorate the tent with markers or crayons. Then cut out the tent, fold it, and put it on a table. Encourage your child to put toy people inside the tent. Then have the toy people celebrate the Feast of Tabernacles by waving palm branches (you can use bay leaves) and having a feast (use fruit-shaped candy or snacks).

Consider using chairs, sheets, and cushions to create a tent that you and your child can sit in. Then pretend to celebrate the Feast of Tabernacles with your child as outlined in Leviticus 23:39-43.

Jesus' Helping Power

Wedding Customs in Bible Times

The Foundation

Jesus wants us to help others.

John 2:1-11

The Background

Hebrew girls could get married at about the age of twelve, while boys often married when they were in their teens. On the evening of the wedding, the young bride was led in a procession from her family's home to the home of the groom's family. The bride wore a veil and was surrounded by her companions. Friends and family marched and carried flowers, torches, and lamps as they walked to the groom's house. When the procession arrived, the guests listened to music and had drinks and food. The couple was crowned with garlands, and parents and friends blessed the couple. A wedding feast was held which could last for several days.

With the backdrop of a wedding celebration, Jesus performed his first miracle. The Lord's presence at the wedding shows us his respect for marriage and the customs surrounding marriage. At the wedding, Mary felt the host's embarrassment when the wine ran out, and she appealed to Jesus to help. Jesus instructed the servants to fill the jars with water, and when the servants drew some out, the water had been changed to wine. Jesus performed his first miracle, and as a result, his disciples put their faith in him.

In this lesson, children will learn that Jesus wants us to help others.

The Tools

- Bible
- plastic tablecloth
- paint smocks
- pitcher
- presweetened, red powdered-drink mix
- wooden spoon

- plastic glasses
- large bowl
- wedding pictures
- plastic dishes, tablecloths, and other items for table settings
- nuts, M&M's candies, raisins
- bowl
- paper cups

The Excavation

Before class, cover a table with a plastic tablecloth. Then fill a large bowl with water. Set out plastic glasses, a wooden spoon, and a pitcher with presweetened, red powdered-drink mix in the bottom. Have paint smocks on hand for children to wear while playing in the water and making the drink mix.

Mix the nuts, M&M's, and raisins together, and put them in a bowl. Set small snack-sized paper cups nearby.

The Project

Ribbon-Cutting

Gather children around the table on which you've placed the large bowl of water, the pitcher with the presweetened, red powdered-drink mix, the wooden spoon, and the plastic glasses.

Say: **Jesus wants us to be helpers! A long time ago, Jesus helped people at a family wedding party. The people at the party drank up all the wine, and there was nothing left to drink! So Jesus told the helpers to fill some jars with water.** Have children put on the smocks. Then direct children to use the plastic glasses to scoop water from the bowl into the pitcher that has the powdered-drink mix in the bottom. Have children stir the mixture.

Then Jesus said, "Pour some of the water out, and give it to the man in charge of the party." Help the children pour some of the drink into their glasses. **Suddenly, the people saw that the water had turned red. The helpers were surprised! The man in charge was surprised!** Ask:

- **What do you think made our water turn red?**

- **How do you think Jesus made the water turn red?**

Say: **I had powdered drink mix in the pitcher before you put the water in. It wasn't a miracle; we just added water to the powdered mix. But Jesus did a real miracle—he turned water into wine! Jesus is powerful, and he** uses his power to help others. Jesus wants you to help others too. Ask:

• [Child's name], who are some people you can help? What kinds of things can you do to help them?

Let the children give examples of ways they can help others.

Whistle While You Work

Say: **Let's sing about Jesus and his helping power.** Sing this song to the tune of "Mary Had a Little Lamb."

Sing

Jesus is my helping power *(show muscles)*,
Helping power, helping power. *(Show muscles.)*
Jesus is my helping power. *(Show muscles.)*
Jesus is my Lord. *(Point up to heaven.)*

My feet walk with helping power *(walk in place)*,
Helping power, helping power. *(Walk in place.)*
My feet walk with helping power. *(Walk in place.)*
Jesus is my Lord. *(Point up to heaven.)*

My hands work with helping power *(wiggle fingers)*,
Helping power, helping power. *(Wiggle fingers.)*
My hands work with helping power. *(Wiggle fingers.)*
Jesus is my Lord. *(Point up to heaven.)*

(Optional verse for older preschoolers)
My mouth speaks his helping power *(point to mouth)*,
Helping power, helping power. *(Point to mouth.)*
My mouth speaks his helping power. *(Point to mouth.)*
Jesus is my Lord. *(Point up to heaven.)*

Blueprint

Have kids sit in a circle, and open your Bible to John 2:1-11. Then say: **One day, Jesus went with his mother and some friends to a wedding celebration.** Show kids some pictures from a wedding. **The wedding was in a town called Cana. People walked from near and far to the wedding.** Have kids put one hand above their eyes and pretend to look around while they walk in place. **The people wanted to see the bride and groom on their wedding day.**

Friends ate food and drank wine. They ate and ate! Encourage the children to pretend to eat food. **Then they drank and drank!** Have the children pretend to drink. **They drank until the wine was all gone. No more wine!** Have kids shake their heads back and forth. **This was such a special day!** "What will we do without any drinks?" thought the man in charge of the wedding.

Mary, Jesus' mother, saw that there was no more wine. "Well, what shall we do?" thought Mary. Have the children hold out their hands and shrug their shoulders. **Turning to Jesus she said, "They have no more wine." Then Jesus' mother talked to the wedding helpers. "Do whatever Jesus tells you," she said.**

One, two, three, four, five, six! Have kids count on their fingers. **Six big stone water jars were nearby. Jesus said to the helpers, "Fill the jars with water."**

So they filled the jars to the top. Then Jesus told the helpers to take some of the liquid out of the jars and give it to the man in charge of the wedding. Encourage kids to pretend to dip a cup in a jar. **The water had turned into wine!** Tell the children to look surprised. **The family at the wedding felt so happy. Jesus had used his power to help them. His helping power saved their wedding party.** Ask:

- **What things does Jesus do to help us?**

- **How do you help out at home?**

- **What things can you do to help clean up our room now?**

Give children jobs to do around your meeting area. For example, kids might straighten up, wipe down your tables, or dust.

Say: **You are great helpers! Thank you for helping me just like Jesus helped the people at the wedding.**

Framework

Have the children gather around one or two tables.

Say: **When people in Bible times got married, they had a big feast, and everybody danced and ate lots of different foods. The feast would sometimes last for several days! Let's set up our own feast right now.**

Let children help get ready for a feast. Have children spread tablecloths over the tables. Provide plastic dishes, and direct children to set a place for each person. The table settings can be as elaborate or simple as you wish. Consider including plastic foods, unlit candles, napkins, pitchers, and trays. Thank children for being such great helpers.

Say: **The people walked, kind of like a parade, to the place where they were going to have the meal. Let's have a big wedding march before we go to the feast we've set up.**

Perform a wedding procession as the people did in biblical times, and often still do in Israel. Allow the children to take turns being the bride and groom in a wedding procession around the room. You might have the bride wear a dress-up veil and the groom wear a Jewish kipa on his head. Have the other children clap and cheer.

Builders Banquet

As children are washing their hands, set out a large bowl of snacks, such as M&M's candies, nuts, and raisins. (Make sure the children do not have food allergies.) Give each child a small cup. Then pray and ask God to bless the snacks, and pray that God will help everyone be a helper to others. Ask:

- **What kinds of food do people eat at weddings?**

Say: **In Bible times, children were given nuts or snacks to eat at weddings. Can you help someone in our class get a wedding snack? Fill a cup with the treats, and give it to someone in the class. Let's help serve each other our snacks.**

Have children take turns serving and helping each other, then let kids enjoy eating the treats.

Dedication

Say: **In Bible times, people gathered together for special times like weddings. While they were together, they blessed each other. To bless someone means to wish that person well. A blessing means that you are special and that God has good plans for you.**

Have two teachers or other adults hold hands as in the game of London Bridge. Direct the children to form a moving line and march under the teachers' arms as you sing the following blessing song to the tune of "Frère Jacques." After the first verse, insert other words, such as "shoulders" or "arms," into the song as indicated. Stop singing at various times during the verses as the teachers trap a child with their arms. Direct everyone to join you in singing the first verse of the blessing song over the child while he or she is "trapped." Be sure that every child is caught and blessed. (Ask parents to come in and help if you need extra assistance with this activity.)

Sing

May the blessing
May the blessing
Of the Lord
Of the Lord

Rest upon your head.
Rest upon your head.
We love you!
We love you!

May the blessing
May the blessing
Of the Lord
Of the Lord
Rest upon your [shoulders, arms, legs, feet].
We love you!
We love you!

Additions

• Bring in a small clay pot (from a craft store) for each child. Put newspapers down over your work area, and give each child a smock or paint shirt. Have children use acrylic paints or markers to decorate their pots.

Tell kids that Jesus has helping power and that he wants us to help others too. Then have children each think of someone who needs help. Ask each child what the person's name is and how the child can help that person. Use a marker to write the person's name on the rim of the child's clay pot. Then write the child's name on the bottom of the pot. Display the pots in an area where they won't be knocked over or broken. The next time you see the children, ask them how they helped the people whose names are written on their pots.

Bible-Town Take-Home Page

Sunday	Monday	Tuesday	Wednesday

Thursday	Friday	Saturday	

Setting the table

Helping to fold the clothes

Making your bed

Sweeping the floor

Picking up toys

Praying for someone

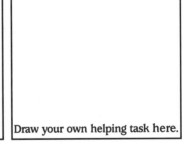

Draw your own helping task here.

Today kids learned about Jesus' miracle at the wedding in Cana. Read John 2:1-11, and remind your child how Jesus turned the water into wine and helped the people at the wedding celebration.

Cut out the helping tasks on this page. Have your child decide which task he or she will do each day next week, and glue the task on that day in the "Helping Calendar." Then have your child decorate the calendar. Post the calendar where your child can see it, and encourage him or her to follow through on helping with the tasks throughout the week.

Scripture Index

Group Publishing, Inc.
Attention: Product Development
P.O. Box 481
Loveland, CO 80539
Fax: (970) 679-4370

Evaluation for
Wee-Built Bible Town

Please help Group Publishing, Inc. continue to provide innovative and useful resources for ministry. Please take a moment to fill out this evaluation and mail or fax it to us. Thanks!

● ● ●

1. As a whole, this book has been (circle one)

not very helpful   very helpful

1   2   3   4   5   6   7   8   9   10

2. The best things about this book:

3. Ways this book could be improved:

4. Things I will change because of this book:

5. Other books I'd like to see Group publish in the future:

6. Would you be interested in field-testing future Group products and giving us your feedback? If so, please fill in the information below:

Name _____

Church Name _____

Denomination _____ Church Size _____

Church Address _____

City _____ State _____ ZIP _____

Church Phone _____

E-mail _____